D1325045

WALKING IN THE
BLACK FOREST

Front Cover - Wutachschlucht

Near Neuweier (Clock Carriers' Way)

WALKING IN THE
BLACK FOREST

BY

FLEUR AND COLIN SPEAKMAN

CICERONE PRESS MILNTHORPE CUMBRIA

© Fleur and Colin Speakman 1990
ISBN 1 85284 050 1

Other Cicerone Guides by Fleur and Colin Speakman:
   King Ludwig Way
   Walking in the Salzkammergut

FOR LYDIA
who loves walking and forests

CONTENTS

FRANCE

KARLSRUHE

● PFORZHEIM

STUTTGART

STRASBOURG

BADEN-BADEN

1

OFFENBURG

Rhine

TRIBERG

FOREST

VILLINGEN

FREIBURG

2

TUTTLINGEN

NEUSTADT

BLACK

BONNDORF

Lake Constance

BASEL
(BASLE)

SWITZERLAND

1. **THE ORTENAUER WINEPATH**
2. **THE CLOCK CARRIERS' WAY**

Walking in the Black Forest

The Black Forest is one of the most famous walking areas in Europe. In fact, it might even be true to say that it was in the Black Forest that the art of long distance walking was invented. The Black Forest Society (Schwarzwaldverein), founded in 1864, is Germany's oldest walking and outdoor organisation and is indeed one of the oldest in Europe. The Westweg is Europe's first waymarked long distance footpath route and dates from 1900, 17 years before the establishment of America's Long Trail and 65 years before England's Pennine Way.

It is because of its excellent network of trails that the Black Forest is so popular for walking. It is not an area of mountains on the scale of the Alps or Pyrenees, but what the Germans call *Mittelgebirge* which is really untranslatable but means middle-ranking hills, not quite mountains but more than mere hills. It is most certainly an area of superb forest, fine ridge walking and, above the Rhine Valley, some magnificent high-level walking with panoramic views. It is also an area of rich history and culture with a fine tradition of hospitality.

This book is intended to provide a brief but practical introduction to the Black Forest for the average English-speaking rambler considering a walking holiday in this beautiful area of Germany.

The book divides into three parts. Part One is called Discovering the Black Forest and intends to whet the appetite for the region; to give someone planning to come to the Black Forest a brief insight into what makes the area special. Part Two is called Planning a Trip and deals with the practicalities of what you need to know before planning a walking holiday in this part of Germany - transport arrangements, maps, equipment, accommodation, food and drink. An important part of this section is a listing and overview of all the offical waymarked routes and packaged walks which are currently available in the Black Forest.

Part Three takes two fine long distance routes, *The Ortenauer Winepath,* and *The Clock Carriers' Way* both of which can be planned easily and conveniently from the UK or USA, with overnight luggage carried each day between accommodation. This is much the best way to enjoy long distance walking for we believe that short day walks from car parks are not what the Black Forest is really about, though countless such opportunities exist. It is in fact perfectly possible to call at local tourist offices throughout the Black Forest to pick up maps and brochures for short circular, waymarked walks from car parks; pleasant family walking perhaps, but not worth travelling all the way to the Black Forest for. The Black Forest Long Distance Routes on the other hand give opportunity to experience the real Black Forest, to understand and share the richness and beauty of a unique part of Europe and the heritage of which these routes now form a part.

Naturally, with everyone who loves long distance walking and great landscapes throughout the world, we share a tremendous debt of gratitude to the Schwarzwaldverein - the Black Forest Society - who over the last 126 years have pioneered the paths and fought to protect this magnificent landscape and its culture in so many different ways, and who have been an inspiration well beyond the boundaries of their native land. Without the Schwarzwaldverein this book would simply not exist.

We would like to express our warmest thanks to the present Chief Executive of the Black Forest Society, Herr Werner Siebler-Ferry, for his kindness and generosity in aiding us with our research for this book. We are grateful too, to Herr Klaus Blum of Triberg, creator of the Clock Carriers' Way for his hospitality, enthusiasm and advice, and to the staff at the tourist offices of Baden-Baden and Offenburg who were particularly helpful to us, and to Mike Buchan, Travel Agent extraordinary who solved the mysteries of a complex itinerary with aplomb. We would also like to record our sincere thanks to Frau Klein at Varnhalt who helped to recover a vital camera (carelessly mislaid) and with it our photographic records.

Finally, we express our gratitude to the people of the Black Forest for their warmth, friendship and hospitality during our visit, proving that tourism, in the right manner, is all about communication between people and increasing mutual understanding.

In the Black Forest, as elsewhere, we share a common heritage.

Fleur and Colin Speakman

PART ONE
Discovering the Black Forest

A Region of Magic and Mystery

The evocative name of the Black Forest or Schwarzwald suggests the spirit of the forest itself in certain dark moods; its magical, mysterious quality when the mist rises out the valleys, enveloping the trees in a shifting veil. At such times the inhabitants sagely nod their heads, declaring 'The witches are brewing up their coffee again.'

Perhaps more surprisingly the western edge of the region, for example around Baden-Baden, Kaiserstuhl and Freiburg, is also a noted wine growing area. In fact so good is the wine that King Louis XIV of France, after waging a particularly bitter campaign against the inhabitants of Baden and laying waste to a considerable area, actually forbade any damage to the vineyards on pain of death - an interesting insight into that monarch's priorities and a tribute to the quality of the wine!

The Black Forest isn't, of course, one single forest, but the name of a region which is covered by a series of forests. It forms the extreme south-west corner of Germany, within the Federal state of Baden-Württemberg, and consists of 7,860 square kilometres of rolling hill country, about 160 km (roughly 100 miles) from north to south and between 60 to 80 km (40-50 miles) east to west. The hills rise up to around 1,500m (about 4,500ft), with much of the land over 1,000m in the form of long, thickly forested ridges. The area is bounded on the west and south by the River Rhine and the French and Swiss frontiers, in the east by the valleys of the Neckar and the Nagold, and in the north by the Kraichgau region beyond Pforzheim.

A Contrasting Landscape

The Black Forest is frequently described as having two distinct areas of contrasting landscape. The northern section has areas of moorland and heath as well as forest and vineyards, while the south has larger areas of forest and scattered farms and is the more scenically dramatic. Much of the charm of the region lies in this distinct contrast.

9

Geologically the region was formed out of ancient rocks, granite and gneiss, but there are also areas of red sandstone which are sometimes dramatically exposed, and which give the forest paths a warm reddish tinge under their carpet of pine needles. The higher reaches of the southern Black Forest are dominated by an immense granite massif through which deep valleys carve their way.

More than half of the Black Forest is carpeted with dense fir, elm and pine woods, but there are equally large tracts of deciduous and mixed woods, interspersed with vivid green grassy tracts and plant-life. Much of the region has large areas of pasture, some arable farmland, orchards around charming farms which in autumn are loaded with fruit, and hamlets, pretty towns and villages rich in historic connections and remains, often featuring delightful little springs or fountains decorated with carved wood, stone or metal.

The sunny western slopes of the Forest open out to countless wine terraces that form fascinating combed, geometrical patterns as you look across to the hills beyond. According to the famous German poet, dramatist and statesman, Wolfgang von Goethe, nowhere else in Germany does the sun seem to shine so brightly or the sky seem so translucent a colour as in the wine region around Ortenau, near the River Rhine.

All-the-year-round Natural Beauty

The Black Forest isn't a National Park or Nature Reserve as such, though substantial areas of the region receive special Protected Landscape' designation from the State Government of Baden-Württemberg. Many areas, such as the Wutachschlucht or the Blin-densee, are formal Nature Reserves where the wildlife has rigorous protection. There are also areas of State or Regional Forest which are rigorously protected too, and local councils have powers and duties to protect the local environment, for example in ensuring new buildings meet appropriate standards.

The Black Forest is an area particularly rich in natural beauty. Though the forest may no longer be natural, having been managed over generations, there is a great variety of woodland and trees of different species and ages permitting a rich undercover of ferns, grasses and wildflowers.

Topinambur flower, Renchtal

Spring and summer bring a dazzling array of wild flowers including alpenroses and gentian in the higher areas, while orchids and heartsease (the charming wild pansies), patches of thyme, harebells, wild iris, the Turk's head lily and the delicate autumn crocus grow in the woodlands. There is also a profusion of butterflies; the Wutachschlucht, for example, boasts about 3000 varieties. The woods also teem with wildlife such as foxes, squirrels, owls, small deer, wild boar, dormice, pine martens and lizards. In and around the woods and streams there is a rich variety of birdlife including woodpeckers, nuthatch and dippers; while out

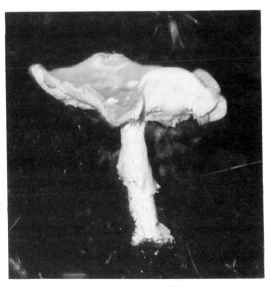

Toadstool, Black Forest

on the open moorland areas, birds of prey such as buzzards and other falcons may be seen hovering.

Autumn, just before the leaves turn into a symphony of gold and russet, is a period of incredible richness in the forest with every conceivable kind of fungi (ranging from those not much larger than pin-heads to those the size of small dinner plates) in a kaleidoscope of milky white, beige, saffron yellow, scarlet, crimson and dull brown through to jet-black. Many varieties are edible, but if you wish to pick your own do take extreme care not to confuse these tempting-looking objects with the poisonous varieties. Late raspberries, bilberries, blackberries, scarlet rowans, elderberries both black and red, sloes, hazelnuts, sweet chestnuts and horse chestnuts provide a feast for the eye. In winter, which in the Black Forest can be long and severe, starting in November and continuing until May with heavy snow-falls that block roads and tracks, the forest becomes a paradise for cross-country skiing - as the many pistes and route marks indicate.

Early Settlement and Development

The original sporadic Celtic settlements of this strategically important area across the Upper Rhine Valley were subjugated by the Romans with a series of military roads which were built through the Forest and by observation towers constructed at high points. One of their achievements was a road through the valley to connect Strasbourg with Rottweil, and the Roman generals soon discovered the pleasures of the hot thermal springs in the areas around Baden-Baden.

The Romans were eventually conquered by a tribe known as the Alemanni who left a distinct mark linguistically on the area but were, in their turn, overcome by the Franks and driven back to the northern uplands. Finally, in the eleventh century, the area was ruled by the Zähringer dynasty of Baden who built many of the market towns such as Freiburg and contributed much to the region's prosperity in the later Middle Ages. What is particularly interesting is that the Zähringer princes were somewhat in advance of their time, preferring to extend their sphere of influence politically without resorting to conquest, and planning their towns such as Villingen, Freiburg and Offenburg as an integrated whole. The Benedictine monasteries

Narrenfigur, Villingen

of Hirsau, Herranalb, St Trudpert (named after an Irish monk), St Märgen and St Blasien - with the aid of the Cistercians (who developed the vineyards) and other monastic orders - helped to develop the region still further. From the thirteenth century to the coming of Napoleon the southern part of the Black Forest came under Austrian rule, with the city of Freiburg as its capital. With Napoleon's victory the Baden area became an arch-dukedom and Württemberg a kingdom instead of a loose collection of regions; a pragmatic device of Napoleon's to ensure there were buffer states between himself and the powerful Austrian Habsburg dynasty. After the Second World War these two regions were united as the State Baden-Württemberg, part of the modern Federal Republic of West Germany.

Life and History
Being so close to both France and Switzerland, these neighbouring cultural influences have helped to shape much of the Black Forest's individual character.

For many centuries, before the coming of the railways and good roads, the central and more mountainous parts of the Black Forest away from the Rhine and Neckar valleys were among the most inaccessible parts of Germany. Villages and farmsteads were scattered and isolated, particularly during the winter months, so that it could often be a two-day journey to fetch a doctor. The region's famous strong liqueurs or schnapps made out of fruit, such as *Kirschwasser* (cherry) or *Mirabelle* (small golden plums), often had to be used medicinally, to dull pain until the doctor arrived.

In common with most upland areas in Europe, the farms were often not sufficiently economically viable to support an entire family unit, and other ways had to be sought. The wood industry, with the allied trades of paper making and furniture making, has always been important in the area. Huge pine trunks were made into enormous rafts and floated down the rivers to saw mills to be made into ships' masts for sailing ships, and over the centuries the Black Forest people became skilled wood carvers, producing not only tools and utensils, but also beautiful carved figures (a tradition perpetuated by the simple carvings on many of the more modern little springs and fountains). This dexterity was to lead to the growth of the clock making industry.

Glass making in the Black Forest originated in the Middle Ages and was initiated by the monasteries and also by particular dukes and princes. It had a very definite effect on the landscape. Quartz was found in abundance, and wood was used in large quantities to make the charcoal to fire the glass.

The preparation or burning of charcoal for the glass or iron industries was an interesting and skilled process. An enormous heap of wood, to a radius of 10m, was built. Logs were propped up vertically against each other and covered with a layer of leaves, grass and moss to make the heap fireproof and reduce draughts. Charcoal pieces from previous burnings were lit in the middle until the heap glowed, making a conical shape as the remaining water in the wood released its steam. It was the charcoal burner's job to make sure that no new holes appeared in the glowing pile, and at the same time to adjust the current of air for an even temperature. The burning took six days and then the kiln was pulled apart to cool off. Around 25% of the original weight of the wood was an average output of charcoal.

The result of this activity was that the original forest of wildwood became partially denuded and, though constantly replaced, the species which tended to be quicker growing (firs and spruces) began to dominate. So the stretches of dark, dense woodland we see in some areas, far from being natural, are the direct result of human activity. Though charcoal burning no longer survives in this form, the name *Kohlenwald* for certain stretches of forest recalls this process. Mining for precious metals such as gold, silver and lead (galena) was also important in past centuries, and traces of these former industries can also be seen on the landscape.

Farming remains important in the Forest, great clearances being created in the valley bottoms for fertile pastureland, sheltered by the thickly wooded ridges. In such clearings you can see the characteristic farmhouses with their immense roofs. It is mostly dairy farming with vast quantities of hay collected from the meadows for storage in the great roof space above the house for feeding to cattle through the long winter. At the Vogtsbauernhof at Gutach you can see a variety of examples at the open air museum of the different types of Black Forest farmhouse, complete with additional store-houses, bake-

Traditional farm with roof barn on the Westweg

houses, a saw-mill and water-mill. Displays of such traditional crafts as blacksmithing, straw basket weaving, charcoal burning and forestry are also included.

The oldest type of *Heidenhaus*, as the earliest type of farmhouse is called, is completely wood-built and its vast roof nearly reaches the ground with the hay loft over the cattle stalls and rooms for the farmhands reached by an outside walkway. Over the main living quarters is the threshing floor, on the upper slope so that the hay cart can be driven straight in. Centuries ago the draught ox who had helped to bring in the vast amount of wood used for the building would be sacrificed and its head hung up outside the first storey to ward off evil spirits and misfortune. Later types of farmhouse changed various details such as giving the house a valley view and a first storey or foundation of stone, thus reducing the risk of fires and making more roof space by re-arrangement of the vast beams. But essentially the farm living quarters were still on level ground at the bottom of the slope, while the hay lofts or barns were conveniently reached on the upper levels of the slope.

There is a certain amount of arable farming in the north, but over to the west vineyards and fruit growing are dominant. It is a wonderful sight to see the clusters of ripening green, black and red grapes with leaves that shade to bronze and crimson; not to mention the outsize apples, pears, plums and, earlier in the season, the famous cherries which have all added so much to the cuisine of the area. In spring there is sometimes the additional magic of a floating sea of white cherry blossom echoed in the still snow-clad peaks of the distance.

Cuckoo Clocks to Orchestrions - The Black Forest Clock Making Industry

It is the glass making industry we have indirectly to thank for the rise of one of the Black Forest's most famous industries. The glass carriers carried glassware on their backs to sell at outlying villages, using a special wooden support covered by a protective trunk-shaped device and bringing back with them other goods discovered on their travels. One of these objects was alleged to be a simple clock which was then imitated in wood, clockwork included. Other historians suggest that an actual wooden clock was brought back by one of the glass carriers in the 1680s and then directly imitated by a skilled local craftsman. The most recent research suggests that the Kreuz brothers built the first wooden clock at their workshop in the Black Forest before 1667. Up till then the only clock in the Black Forest was reputed to have been the sun, though Strasbourg and Augsburg had long been famous as clock making centres.

From such modest beginnings, within 200 years the Black Forest clock making industry grew to be a worldwide business with an annual turnover of 1.8 million clocks in 1870, supplying Europe and the rest of the world with robust, cheap, practical and reliable clocks. The rise of this industry is a fascinating story of the skill and ingenuity of the Black Forest people who, using the simplest raw material to hand, namely wood, created something that would prove to be such a source of wealth.

The early stages of the industry were slow and uncertain. The first production period (1670-1720) was sporadic in terms of output. It was only after the Franco-Austrian wars, when peace had been restored, that a number of men in the north-west area of the Black Forest started to build wooden clocks on a serious scale: Simon Dilger in Urach, Franz Ketterer in Schönwald, Michael Dilger in Neukirch and Matthais Löffler in Gütenbach all started up in business in their small factory-workshops. Apprentices and journeymen were taken on and, once they became masters in their turn, they set up independently so that clock making spread apace and rapidly began to outgrow its cottage industry origins.

The early clocks were made entirely of wood - case, wheels, hands and even the cogs and spindles (using hardwood), with a simple stone out of the fields for a weight. These clocks had a single hand and only told hours. However technical developments such as a minute hand, glass weights and bells, wooden bells, wooden spindles with metal cogs, and hand and bells made out of bronze, soon became the order of the day. The clock mechanism was originally regulated by a balance which swivelled, then by a cowtail pendulum and finally by use of a long and short pendulum in the familiar pine-cone style.

Clock making was originally broken down into a number of different stages, often with women and girls providing the stylised painted decoration of the face (usually of flowers, but also of animals or simple rural scenes). Originally the clock face was a simple wooden one with painted numbers, but these became increasingly artistic and could be made of painted paper, wood, glass and metal. The next step was to produce a clock capable of striking the quarter and half hours.

Franz Ketterer of Schönwald is generally credited as producing the first cuckoo clock. Originally the cuckoo (whose 'call' was constructed on the bellows principle) popped out of an aperture from a simple tree painted on the face of the clock. Many decades later the cuckoo began to inhabit an elaborately carved home. The idea caught on and became a huge popular success, and cuckoo clocks were built in vast numbers in Switzerland as well as the Black Forest. They are still made and sold in large quantities - Triberg is a major centre - mostly mass produced for the tourist market, but it is still possible to buy hand-crafted pieces of exceptional quality and charm.

Sometimes a simple tune was played and this mechanism, in time, came to be capable of more complex melodies. Further developments were mechanical figures which did a number of ingenious things, such as a dumpling-eating man, marching figures or a smith striking an anvil; mechanical musical boxes that could play a series of tunes; and finally the elaborately engineered *Orchestrion,* a vast instrument which often had a repertoire of tunes played on the instruments of a mechanical orchestra and at its height had music specially composed for it by contemporary composers. Sadly this brilliant technology, which reached its zenith before the First World War, was rapidly challenged and overtaken by Edison's phonograph, the gramophone, the juke box and the modern hi-fi record player.

The Black Forest craftsmen were men who often had a number of technical skills at their disposal such as wood carving, metal working, carpentry and musical instrument making. By 1780 clock bells were already being exported to England and Holland. The early, fragile glass bells for striking the quarters (a relic of the old glass making industry) were replaced by metal in the later decades of the eighteenth century. By the mid-nineteenth century about 50% of the total clock making production was for the popular household 24-hour clock with its lacquered wooden face and chiming mechanism. By 1810 the annual turnover of Black Forest clocks was between 150,000 to 200,000 clocks, and by 1840 this had reached 600,000. It was also estimated that by this period 5,000 people were occupied in some branch of the industry, with the addition of about 1,000 clock dealers who actually sold the goods. Before this period production had been largely domestic with one master worker employing one or two assistants and various members of the family helping too.

As local markets became saturated other markets for surplus clocks had to be found, so the clock makers started to carry their wares to other towns and villages in and around the Black Forest. But it obviously made sense for the clock makers to employ other people to do their selling for them, so dealers bought up a range of clocks and became known as 'packers' because they packed up such a large quantity of goods. A single Schörenbach clock packer sent over 21,000 clocks between 1821-1864 to London and Hamburg. There undoubtedly was tension at times between clock makers and the packers, or clock carriers, who were accused of exploiting the clock makers' skill.

But it was the Black Forest clock carriers, using many of the old glass carriers' original routes and tracks through the Forest, who became one of the most characteristic features of the industry. They sometimes formed themselves into groups to travel in company as it was risky business to travel alone with cash about one's person. The clock carrier would arrive in a town or village, hire a room for a few days and set out to sell his wares in the neighbourhood like a travelling pedlar. This would occur not only in towns and villages, but even in the most outlying areas. The characteristic figure of the clock carrier in his white stockings, knee-breeches, broad-brimmed hat and with his colourful pack of clocks on his back (carried on a wooden support called a *Krätze*) can still be seen in illustrations and in folk museums such as the one at Triberg. One of the most delightful walking routes in the Black Forest - The Clock Carriers' Way, described in Part Three of this book - is dedicated to keeping the memory of these intrepid explorers and entrepreneurs alive.

Eventually the distances covered by the clock carriers grew longer and spread to the Breisgau on the French border, the Rhine Valley, Alsace, Württemberg and Switzerland. Later still they reached Cologne, Holland and England, Hungary, Turkey, Russia, Poland, Denmark, Sweden, Italy, Spain and Portugal. A special clock was presented to Catherine the Great of Russia and close trade links resulted. Particular clock carriers specialised in particular countries and the clocks were often specially made and decorated in the style popular in that country. Having conquered Europe, it was only a matter of time before the Black Forest clock reached the Near East and North America. One Schwarzwald emigré, Joseph Kirner, achieved such success and became so wealthy that an American town in North Carolina is named after him - Kernesville.

Sadly the clock trade became a victim of its own success. An American clock dealer decided that demand could be satisfied with machine-made clocks and loaded a ship with them and set sail for Hamburg. The competition was a severe blow to the Black Forest clock trade. In 1850 the Archduke of Baden founded the Clock Making College at Furtwangen which is still in existence and now the home of the famous German National Clock Museum. Its first Principal was Robert Gerwig, the brilliant railway engineer and builder of the Black Forest Railway through Triberg, who saw to it that youngsters learnt not only clock making but allied technology as well. He also arranged that any additional materials needed, apart from the wood which was of course available in abundance, should not be obtained from abroad but, if possible, from within Germany itself in order to cut costs and encourage home industry. The Black Forest clock trade also fought back by studying its competition, particularly in the case of Junghans who adapted American production methods to German expertise so that his factory rose to be the largest of its kind in Europe before the outbreak of the First World War.

Technical skill was again greatly in demand during the Second World War, and much sophisticated weaponry depended on the clock maker's precision - all the deadly armoury of rockets, bombs and U-boats. Thankfully, since the Second World War the skills of the Black Forest people have been put to much greater use for the benefit of men - for medical equipment, for the optics, photographic and cinematic industries, and above all for the modern technology of computers and electronics.

Wine Making

A second major characteristic activity in the Black Forest is wine making, probably introduced to the region by the Romans and certainly mentioned by writers on the region in the eighth century. Vines need several factors in order to produce wines of quality and these are the correct soil in which to grow the grapes, the right kind of climate (good, dry summers), the right type of grape and vintners with good technical expertise.

White wine is generally produced from the green grapes and keeps it light colour (*Sylvaner* and *Riesling* are typical), being separated from the grape skins at an early stage and then being pressed. The rosé wine uses black grapes, but the pink colour comes from the fact that there is only contact with the grape skins for 24 hours with no tannin content, and it is bottled young and then drunk (*Weißherbst* is the most common type from the region). Red wine, also from black grapes, has a longer contact with the grape skins and a more full-bodied flavour (*Spätburgunder* is a good example). Most popular of all are the white wines and probably the best known is the *Riesling*, an elegant wine. The *Ruländer* is a fiery wine with a definite bouquet from a vine which grows well in the Kaiserstuhl area. Less heavy, but a near relative, is the *Weiße Burgunder*. Other wines with a herby and rose-scented bouquet are the *Traminer* and the *Gewürtztraminer*. Most popular in the Baden area is the *Müller-Thurgau* with its light muscatel flavour, which should be drunk young. Most noteworthy of the red wines is *Baden Spätburgunder*, often considered by the connoisseur as one of the best red wines in the world, full-bodied with the aroma of bitter almonds.

The great delight of visiting the Black Forest, and particularly in walking through or near to its vineyards (for example along the Ortenauer Winepath described in Part Three), is that you can sit down in your hotel or *Gasthof* after a day's walk through the vineyards and order a carafe or bottle of the excellent local wines which you have seen ripening in the sun earlier in the day. Much of this is unavailable for export, so you can enjoy a local speciality along with the region's first class food. German wine has an undeserved reputation for being sweet and uninteresting, partially owing to the vast quantities produced for British supermarkets. Nothing could be further from the truth!

The cheapest wine in Germany is ordinary *Tafelwein* (tablewine) or *Landwein* (similar in quality but from a particular region). This is usually quite acceptable, particularly with food, but it is worth paying just a little more for a very much better product.

The *Qualitätswein mit Prädikat (QmP)* label on a bottle (or sometimes in wine growing regions by the carafe, excellent value for money), is wine of the best quality with no added sugar. The scale then continues to *Kabinett* which is generally a wine of some fruitiness, but also dry and elegant, followed by *Spätlese* (late harvest) which is a particularly well balanced wine and the *Auslese* which has an even richer bouquet, followed by the *Beerenauslese,* an extremely fine quality wine. The list is completed with two very expensive, but superb wine categories, *Trockenbeerauslese* which has a wonderful sweet taste after the grapes have actually started to rot and is considered by the connoisseurs as creating some of the finest wines in the world, and culminating in the even rarer *Eiswein* when the grapes are actually touched by frost and make a particularly exquisite dessert wine. *Qualitätswein (QbA)* does have sugar added, but the skill is in balancing acidity and sweetness to compensate for climate vagaries and the sugar is in fact added to increase the alcohol content as well as to increase the level of sweetness. Germany has a rigorous wine testing system and awards of bronze, silver and gold are given by independent bodies.

In former times oak vats were used in the wine making process and everything was done by hand - you often see old fashioned wine presses and oak vats outside farmhouses used for flower baskets or decoration. Nowadays the oak vats have given way to stainless steel and plastic with hygiene standards rigorously enforced. Both EEC laws and the German government regulations have to be stringently observed. The central organisation is the Zentralle Badische Winser-

*Bocksbeutel
with
Affentaler wine*

genossenschaft (ZBW) in Breisach and is the largest and most modern in Europe.

Baden is one of the few regions in Germany allowed to bottle some wines, such as the *Affentaler* in the famous triangular *Bocksbeutel* shape which is also used for Frankish wines. The climate in Baden is particularly good and it is one of the most beautiful wine growing areas in Germany, especially the Ortenau, Breisgau, Kaiserstuhl and Tunnisberg areas with their fertile soils (volcanic in origin), and the Markgräfenland in the southern Black Forest which has the *Gutedel* as a typical wine, light, delicate with a mild bouquet and often sold in inns from the cask. The wine area from Freiburg to Offenburg has wine mainly for local use, whilst the Glottertal specialises in *Spätburgunder* and *Weißherbst*. Many local wine festivals take place in early autumn in towns and villages around the Black Forest which encourage guests to try the new wine at innumerable stalls where you buy your glass with your first drink and carry it round for further samplings. It is traditional to eat warm *Zwiebelkuchen* with new wine (also known as *Süsswein* or *Weinmost*), the newly fermented and cloudy grape juice of the wine harvest. Zwiebelkuchen is rather like a French onion tart or quiche and can be delicious when the pastry is particularly light; chopped chives are sometimes added or even finely chopped bacon.

Colourful Customs

Customs, folk traditions and their related costumes are also very much part of the way of life in the Black Forest.

The spectacular *Bollenhut* (a traditional hat) has become for many a symbol of the region, but it is worth remembering that it really comes from the Gutachtal and that every valley has its own traditional costume. This was usually special wear for church and other important occasions. The women in particular have some eye-catching confections. The Bollenhut consists of eleven large red pompons worn on a creamy white straw hat (married women wear black pompons), and under the hat is a stiff black lace veil and black cap. A full dark skirt with white puff-sleeved blouse, black flower-embroidered velvet bodice with glittering collar and a black silk pinafore complete the ensemble. Traditionally the plaited hair at the back is covered by a waterfall of coloured glass beads.

The *Schäppel* is another head-dress, this time made out of hundreds of glass beads and ribbons, shaped rather like a drum. The glass blowing industry undoubtedly helped to influence this headgear, as did the popularity of the Virgin Mary's crown in baroque times which became adapted as a sort of bridal crown. Both the Bollenhut and the Schäppel are weighty affairs, but original period pieces can look very dignified and striking.

Fasnet or *Fastnacht* is the Black Forest version of the Shrovetide or pre-Lenten carnivals with its rituals in some cases going back to pre-Christian times. Winter and attendant evil spirits are driven out by the use of masks, costumes and noise. Traditional Fasnet costumes are generally made up of small, coloured tags of material stitched together on basic trousers and top, but particular areas have adopted their own individual jester personalities and witch-style or even animal masks. Some of the most striking costumes are covered in snail shells or walnut shells or even in a more modern variant, playing cards. At Oberkirch (which you pass on the Ortenauer Winepath), the masks have a rather poignant significance and seventeenth century origin as the young girls would wear some particularly hideous masks in an attempt to deter the boisterous soldiery as they went through the town during the period of the Thirty Years War. But in the spirit of carnival today they no longer awaken these darker memories. In fact so strong and uninhibited is the pleasure in having fun and dressing in appropriate style, that a large number of the towns in the Black Forest are formed into Jester Fraternities and have their own *Narrenfigur* (Fool) who has his own special dialect name such as *Schnürri* or *Gags*. Wolfach and Villingen have good collections of old carnival masks while special Fastnet museums in Bad Dürrheim and Kenningen give further fascinating insights. Parades, balls, satirical sketches on town events and personalities and a good deal of exuberance are all an integral part of every Fasnet occasion.

Fasnet is only one part of the rich heritage of customs, traditions and folktales. Where but in Germany would the inhabitants of one small town sit down to a meal once a year of a splendid *Wurst* (sausage) more than 10m (over 30ft) in length? This in fact happens at Katherine's Market or Kätarlesmarkt at Seelbach and recalls an ancient rising by a group of peasants against their noble overlord for trying to exact his tithes by force. The peasants were led by the son of the Vogt, a man who acted as steward to the nobleman and who was also in love with the nobleman's daughter, Katherine. She obviously reciprocated this feeling and was deeply distressed when her sweetheart and 16 of his rebellious companions were captured by her father's soldiers and imprisoned deep in his dungeon. Desperately she thought of some way of buying their freedom and finally advised the 17 men to offer her father a large quantity of their particular kind of Wurst of which he was inordinately fond. To their great joy the nobleman agreed to this bargain, and one ell of sausage was demanded for each man. Thus the length of the sausage was 17 ells, over 10m (30ft) in length. So every year in Katharine's honour this magnificent Wurst is eaten at a ceremonial meal at the fair.

Another delightful Black Forest story concerns Hornberg, an old town north of Triberg, served by the Schwarzwaldbahn (Black Forest Railway). Some centuries ago the townspeople wanted to honour the visit of the local duke by firing off the cannon in his honour. A lookout gave the signal as he saw in the distance the dust of what he thought was the duke's entourage. The shots were duly fired, but the cloud of dust proved to be a herd of cattle. A second false alarm was also given and even a third, so when the duke really arrived the inhabitants had no gunpowder left for their cannon and were reduced to shouting 'Bang' and 'Piff, Paff, Pouf!' The duke became angry, thinking the people were disrepectfully mocking him till the matter was tactfully explained. Since then, if any long-planned event degenerates into a fiasco, local people say 'It's like the Hornberg Schießen.' It's also an example of real life sounding remarkably like an operatic libretto!

Railways

The southern Black Forest is as much a paradise for the rail enthusiast as the walker. The Schwarzwaldbahn (Black Forest Railway) runs from Offenburg, on the Karlsruhe-Basle main line, to Konstanz via Triberg through the centre of the Black Forest. Its construction, between 1863 and 1873, was a triumph of civil engineering. It climbs to 832m above sea level, and between Hornberg and Sommerau has no less than 36 tunnels, totalling 9.5 km in length. The engineer of the line was Robert Gerwig (1820-85) who went on to build not only another of the Black Forest's famous lines, the Höllentalbahn, but also the world famous St Gotthard line in Switzerland.

The building of the Schwarzwaldbahn was at first considered to be technically impossible. It was begun in 1862, but it took some time for the definitive route to be decided. Finally the chosen route went through the Gutach Valley, even though this was the most technically demanding of the suggested routes. Severe problems of gradient and curvature had to be overcome. The solution became an inspiration and highpoint of nineteenth century railway engineering, using two double loops partly in the tunnel to cope with the enormous change in level. These double loops were the prototype for many subsequent mountain railways throughout the world, including the St Gothard. This route is breathtaking - small but powerful electric locomotives climbing their way through a landscape of deep valleys, mountains, splendid panoramas, cliffs, rushing streams, waterfalls, lakes, woodland, farms and small towns. A trip over the section between Offenburg and Villingen is an experience not to be missed.

The Höllentalbahn, from Neustadt to Freiburg, was completed in 1877, with an extension from Donauechsingen in 1901. It follows a line of perpendicular cliffs in the Höllental, climbing tortuous gradients so steep that you see the line of carriages tilt as they ascend from Hinterzarten over the summit into the Höllental, a wide valley formed in the Ice Age.

In 1934 The Dreiseenbahn (Three Lakes Line) was built. This branch from the Höllentalbahn at Titisee to Seebrugg through the Bärental, passing the lakes at Titisee, Windgfällweiher and the Schluchsee, is the highest standard-gauge railway in Germany (rising to 937m above sea level near Feldberg).

The Wutachtalbahn is the fourth of the celebrated Black Forest railways and is perhaps the most spectacular of all. It runs from Zollhaus-Blumberg to Weizen, a distance of 26 km. It was originally planned as a branch of the Schwarzwaldbahn with six tunnels, including a remarkable turning tunnel and a spiral tunnel. There were also four large viaducts. The line was particularly important for military purposes, providing a route which did not have to go through neutral Switzerland. It is now kept open only as a preserved *Museumbahn* (steam railway) with trains operating to a special time-table on certain dates during the summer months.

There's also an interesting preserved line from Kandern to Haltingen through the Kandern Valley which uses a mixture of steam and diesel, and the little Acherntalbahn which runs from Achern to Offenhöfen via Kappelrodeck (see the Ortenauer Winepath, Day Two). This operates with ordinary diesel rail-cars during the week but provides a service hauled by historic steam locomotives on certain Sundays between May and October.

The Schwarzwaldverein - The Black Forest Society

In 1864 a group of people in Freiburg decided that the as yet undiscovered Black Forest should become better known for the recreation and tourist opportunities the area offered, so they founded the Badische Schwarzwaldverein, soon to be called more simply the Schwarzwaldverein (Black Forest Society). In 1884 a similar organisation was formed in Stuttgart, known as the Württembergische Schwarzwaldverein.

In 1934 the two organisations, from Baden and from Württemberg, which now had a total of 151 District Groups between them, joined forces at a meeting in Lenzkirch as a single Schwarzwaldverein. Not only did this new, enlarged Society continue to open many new footpath routes, but it began to play an increasingly important role in environmental protection. Major battles have taken place in recent years, such as those to save the Wutachschlucht from flooding, for a hydro-electric scheme and to prevent the building of new motorways across the heart of the Black Forest.

The Society now boasts over 92,000 members, with 237 District Groups and 63 Youth Groups. It has a total of 23,000 km of way-marked footpath under its care, from the famous High-level Routes first marked out some 90 years ago, to local Link Paths in different districts. Over 7,600 rambles were organised by the Society's various groups in 1988 with 195,000 people taking part.

The Black Forest Society is Germany's oldest and second largest walking and outdoor organisation and has recently celebrated its 125th anniversary. It is interesting to see what an organisation with such a long and distinguished history regards as its priorities today. The Society sees itself as helping to protect and conserve this beautiful area which is situated so close to some of Europe's largest industrial conurbations in Germany, France and Switzerland. The emphasis of the Society's work has therefore changed; whilst it still campaigns to keep the area open for walkers, it is now also dedicated to ensuring that visitor pressure does not erode that precious environment. The Society's President, Dr Hermann Person, has warned about the environmental hazards from the 'avalanche of tin' (namely the cars which flood the picturesque landscape) and the additional threat posed by a relative newcomer where 'hardly a footpath seems safe from the deadly mountain bikes.'

The Society is also dedicated to helping to maintain the way of life, customs and traditions of the area and to developing an awareness among young people of the natural world and pleasures of the countryside. Its particular concern with all aspects of environmental protection of the area also includes support for scientific investigation of threatened species, the Forest's ecological systems and related matters.

The famed High-level Routes from Pforzheim to Basle, Waldshut, and Schaffhausen are criss-crossed by innumerable Traverse Routes clearly marked by a sophisticated range of symbols. The Black Forest Society is able to protect this very large area by making use of its network of District Groups and Youth Groups, the latter not only having an active walking and skiing programme, but also being much involved with traditional folk dancing and singing in traditional regional costume. But most particularly the young people take a very active role in environmental protection.

As well as looking after its 23,000 km of footpaths, the Schwarzwaldverein takes care of bridges, steps, benches, viewing towers and a chain of hostels; work which all takes a major slice of its voluntary manpower and annual budget. Like any voluntary body much of its campaigning work had to be done by persuasion. About half the Black Forest is owned by various kinds of public and private consortia, a third is purely privately owned and the rest belongs to the State. Agreement has to be sought about creating new routes. The Black Forest Society has to wage a constant battle against the surfacing of paths with tarmac as new roads are built to meet the demands of cars and of visitor pressure. It is expensive and time consuming to re-route paths and of course not always possible, so the number of routes would inevitably shrink dramatically without the constant vigilance of the Black Forest Society.

Many volunteers help to keep down the cost, in a similar way to voluntary wardens in British National Parks who also patrol and work for the countryside on an unpaid basis. The Society is very much a campaigning organisation which has not hesitated to fight strenuously, for example against the proposed motorway through the Black Forest in the 60s despite the extreme pressure for the new road from hoteliers and many other commercial and official organisations.

The Society also produces detailed maps of the region (in conjunction with the Landvermessungsamt of Baden-Württemberg) which mark all the main paths, places of refreshment and the like, and it also has produced some excellent guidebooks for the walker. Members not only get a fully illustrated quarterly magazine which airs important environmental issues, but a comprehensive walking programme under expert guides and the choice of staying at a number of well-run hostels for a comparatively modest outlay. An interesting question that the Society posed itself in early days is still valid. Is the Black Forest Society merely an organisation which happens to be situated IN the Black Forest or is it an organisation FOR the Black Forest? The answer lies surely in the fact that this is a very special region which is very vulnerable and easily endangered and has something unique to offer the visitors from all over the world as well as its local communities.

The battle for the Wutachschlucht, the dramatic scenic gorge set in miles of woodland landscape (see Clock Carriers' Way, Day Five), was fought to preserve this unique area of great importance for the naturalist against developing reservoir facilities. It became a historic battle in which ordinary citizens campaigned by means of posters, press conferences and pamphlets, thus becoming a forerunner of the grass-roots movements of the 70s and 80s in which citizens' action groups waged successful campaigns against an embattled bureaucracy. The Society was also able to curtail the scale and building of new cable-cars and chair-lifts which also play their part in gouging out large areas of landscape and doing untold long-term ecological damage.

In 1981 action was taken to ensure that the Black Forest woodland remained mixed forestry, as opposed to single species quick growing conifers, and there was also a successful campaign against developing the upper reaches of the Rhine and Lake Constance to make them more accessible to shipping. In 1982 the Schwarzwaldverein and the Foresters' Organisation joined forces against what they described as 'the 4 v's' that threatened the integrity of the Black Forest" *Verstraßen, Vertrassen, Verdrahten,* and *Verbauen* - in other words opposition to the development of too many roads, too much tarmac, too much wire fencing and too much indiscriminate new building in the Black Forest. The impact of car exhaust pollution causing acid rain and decimation of the woodland has led to another major recent campaign.

As elsewhere in Europe, and indeed throughout the world, protection of the environment of the Black Forest is an investment for the future of mankind, for without a balance between the conflicting demands placed upon our environment, there can be no future. Excellent as the work of the Black Forest Society is, the future of this beautiful area will be determined as much outside as within its boundaries. Such threats as acid rain - which could destroy the forests - and the greenhouse effect are no respecters of national frontiers. This means an awareness and sense of purpose by individuals and governments on an international scale, for no nation exists in isolation; its economic and industrial activities and emissions have global ecological implications which can neither be avoided nor evaded.

PART TWO

Planning a Trip to the Black Forest

Getting to the Black Forest

Travel to the Black Forest gets easier each year. Undoubtedly the most civilised way, and the one we recommend, is by rail. If you are travelling from the UK, BR's new Channel Train service offers excellent overnight facilities from London, the North or the Midlands via Harwich-Hoek van Holland, leaving the previous afternoon by Channel Train or Provincial Express to Harwich and catching the Inter-city Express (Colonia) from Hoek to Köln. From Köln there is an excellent connection on Euro-City direct to Karlsruhe, Baden-Baden or Freiburg from where local trains link into almost every medium-sized town in the Black Forest. You will certainly be at your hotel or guest-house, close to your chosen start at almost any point in the Black Forest for any long distance walk, well before your evening meal with plenty of time to change and even explore the area beforehand.

The range of bargain leisure tickets now offered by German Federal Railways (Deutsche Bundesbahn) are available from British Rail International (Victoria Station, London SW1 071-834-2345) and BR International ticket agencies and are valid from any railway station within the UK via Channel Train (the new name for boat-train services even before the opening of the Channel Tunnel). These make air travel distinctly uncompetitive in price, especially if there are two or more people in your party when considerable reductions are available. You can also get a bargain-priced Black Forest Tourenkarte, valid on local trains and buses throughout the area, if you arrive in the region by train from outside Germany. This is purchased before you leave.

Another advantage of coming by rail is the actual journey alongside the Rhine Valley, past Koblenz and the Lorelei, which is scenically spectacular, particularly if enjoyed from a DB dining car, a treat not to be enjoyed by motorists on the high-level motorway behind

Typical Black Forest farm - Clock Carrier's Way

Forest track, near Unterkirnach

juggernauts or by air travellers lost in the clouds. (BR offices and international ticket agencies will give further details.)

Should you prefer to fly, there are good connecting train services from Stuttgart or Basle into the Black Forest and even a taxi service if pre-booked. Motorists can probably make the Black Forest in a day from the Channel Ports if they make an early start or take an overnight boat. Train travel is a lot less stressful, does less harm to the environment and given the excellence of local rail services and linking bus networks within the Black Forest, not to mention the superb scenery to be enjoyed through the carriage or bus window, the car is no real advantage. In fact a car is more likely to be a worry and liability to park and leave when walking.

There is a very good combined pocket rail and bus timetable available from stations in the Black Forest. This is published by Deutsche Bundesbahn and covers all local train and bus services. Many of these services run parallel to walking routes, useful if fatigue or bad weather make you seek an alternative form of transport. You will find almost all the local train services in the Black Forest, including the Schwarzwaldbahn, in the Thomas Cook European Timetable.

Terrain, Climate, Equipment and Maps

Because the Black Forest is criss-crossed by such an excellent network of paths and trails which are generally in good condition and well surfaced, the walking, certainly by British standards, can generally be described as easy. If there is a disadvantage it is that many farm tracks or terraces through vineyards have been surfaced, and even though they are traffic-free and often very delightful walking, they can be hard on the feet, particularly in warm weather. There are ascents but they tend to be gradual rather than steep, and anyone who is used to typical British hill country will find little problem. Much walking is in the shelter of the forest which makes the ways cool in summer and sheltered if the weather is poor.

Lightweight boots are ideal for most Black Forest terrain, the kind that you can wear comfortably all day, giving support but without being too heavy on the feet over distance.

Climate in the Black Forest is typical of Central Europe, which means severe winters, usually with heavy snowfall between mid-November and the end of April when paths are likely to be blocked. Walking is not recommended in this period unless it is the version with skis (cross-country skiing or Langlaufen). Summers are generally dry and warm, with the hottest temperatures in July and August when walking in some areas can be uncomfortable with temperatures approaching the mid-20s Centigrade (80s Fahrenheit). The best walking months are therefore late spring and early summer (late May, June) and again in late summer and early autumn (September, October). September is actually a peak month for walking holidays so accommodation is often full and pre-booking is essential.

Though it is not a mountain area, altitudes of up to 1,500m cause sharp fluctuations in temperatures which even in summer can fall quickly with sudden storms and rainy periods. Mist soon covers the thickly forested summit ridges, and it is then you discover why it is called the 'Black' Forest. It is a good idea to always have a compass with you - wayfinding in such conditions can be difficult, and it is easy to get lost in a forest or vineyard landscape without too many obvious waymarks.

Take warm clothing with you at any time of the year - weatherproof jacket, waterproof over-anorak and spare sweater, though it is worth having a pair of shorts or light skirt in your rucksack to change into once the temperatures begin to rise (plus sun-hat, particularly through the vineyards which can be very hot indeed). Do remember to keep a small first aid pack in your equipment so that you always have essentials to hand.

Good as waymarking is in the Black Forest, it is by no means perfect. There are gaps, in some cases where waymarks have been stolen or damaged, in other cases where they are ambiguous, or hard to spot, and a good map is therefore essential.

There is a good choice of maps available at 1:50,000 and some at 1:25,000 scale. Undoubtedly the most accurate and most strongly recommended by the Black Forest Society is the series of 1:50,000 maps with a blue cover, produced jointly by the Black Forest Society and the Landvermessungsamt Baden-Württemberg. This series has all the up-to-date information including all the Society's official waymarked routes. They are accurate and reliable (broadly similar to the Landranger Ordnance Survey sheets in the UK) and perfectly adequate for most well marked routes. They cover the entire Black Forest in a series of ten sheets and are available from local bookshops in the Black Forest area or in advance either direct from the Schwarzwaldverein (prepayment in Dm with your order - address below), or in the UK from Stanfords, 27a Floral Street, London, WC2 9LP.

The Schwarzwaldverein (Black Forest Society) publish a number of other useful maps and guides (in German), including guides to several of the long distance routes. Details of these routes, including that of their network of hostels, can be obtained by writing to the Schwarzwaldverein e.V., Haupgeschäftsstelle, Rathausgasse 33, 7800 Freiburg in Breisgau, Germany.

Accommodation

One of the real joys of the Black Forest is the excellent range of accommodation available, from simple hostels to four-star hotels offering every luxury. Anyone planning to walk one of the High-level Routes or longer Traverse Routes can use the Schwarzwaldverein hostels (reduction for membership of the SV) or the Naturfreundehäuser. There are also several DJH Youth Hostels in the area available to anyone with an International YHA card.

Information about the numerous campsites in the Black Forest can be obtained from the local tourist information centres and from the Fremdenverkehrsverband, Schwarzwald, Bertoldstraße 45, Postfach 1660, 7800 Freiburg, in Breisgau, Germany (Tel: 0761 271 3390).

You can either plan your route by booking in advance before leaving home, or by making a reservation each night by telephone for the next day's walk ahead. This can be problematic in September when accommodation is at a premium. The Black Forest Tourist Association (Fremdenverkehrsverband Schwarzwald, address above publishes a comprehensive accommodation guide).

One way of avoiding the hassle of pre-booking your accommodation separately from outside Germany and worrying about carrying luggage or a heavy rucksack, is to take one of the excellent *ohne Gepäck* packages which are bookable in advance. We give details of all those currently available and recommended by the Baden-

Württemberg Tourist Office later in this section.

Food and Drink

One reason to take a walking holiday in the Black Forest is to enjoy the food which in the Black Forest can, almost without exception, be described as excellent. There is also the consoling thought that if you are tackling a long distance walk, you can feel a little less guilty about calories at the end of an energetic day!

You will rarely find yourself more than a couple of hours' walk from a Gasthaus in the Black Forest - loosely translated as an inn but more accurately as an inn-restaurant which usually also has accommodation. These generally serve excellent food and drink from mid-morning until late evening. However, they also close on one day a week (Ruhetag) which can cause problems if you arrive at that particular time in a small village or hamlet with no other Gasthaus. If you are tackling a long day with no main settlements en route around lunchtime and you are not sure of the Ruhetag, some emergency rations (nuts, chocolate, fruit) in the bottom of a rucksack might be a wise precaution.

Even though in an era of the low pound compared with the Deutschmark, eating out is not unduly expensive in Germany (somewhat cheaper on average than the UK). You may, however, feel a need to keep within a tight budget on a walking holiday and here most towns and villages have well supplied supermarkets where, if you want to save costs at midday, bread, cakes, biscuits, cold meats, fruit and drinks can be purchased.

If you enjoy a decent glass of beer on a ramble, most Black Forest Gasthäuser will supply just that. Germany is the land of superb beers, all brewed under the sixteenth century purity laws (Reinheitsgebot) which require that only hops, malt and water can be used in the making. The Black Forest region is no exception with over 60 local breweries brewing an estimated 6,000 varieties of beer and ale which vary from the strong and bitter to the soft and light. Wine is always available, and of course soft and non-alcoholic drinks, including the popular Apfelsaft (apple juice), Traubensaft (grape juice), or Johannisbeersaft (blackcurrant juice), proprietary soft drinks and local mineral water. You might like to try Apfelschorle as a variation, a refreshing mixture of Apfelsaft and mineral water, particularly thirst quenching on a hot day.

The variety, quality and appetising presentation of food make all mealtimes in the Black Forest something to look forward to. For breakfast (Frühstuck) you can expect a delicious variety of cold meats thinly sliced, including the superb local ham (Schinken) which can be either of a cooked variety or cured, rather like the Italian prosciutto. A variety of cheeses are usually available, lightly boiled eggs, butter and the most delicious preserves either black cherry or Waldfrüchte (literally fruits of the forest) and the famous Black Forest honey, a dark amber colour, known as Waldhonig (forest honey) or sometimes even Tannenhonig (fir tree honey). Breads appear in all their variety from crusty rolls to various rye breads, wholewheat bread, crisp breads and sometimes a brioche-type loaf. Tea and coffee are always available, but remember the tea is much less strong than the varieties normally used in England and will appear rather weak as the Germans tend to drink it without milk (schwarz) or with lemon, and though milk for tea is available it produces an insipid mixture. Cereals, yoghurt, fruit juice and fresh fruit are usually on offer as well and it is customary to help yourself from an attractively laid out buffet.

Lunch (Mittagessen) may be as much or as little as you please. Many Germans make lunchtime their main meal so that your best value in a Gasthaus will usually be the Tagesmenu or Tageskarte, though almost invariably there is a choice of the table d'hote. But if you prefer to have a snack, especially if you are walking and wish to keep lunch light so that you can do justice to a good meal in the evening, ask for the Vesperkarte (snack menu) or study the Vesper section in the menu. Here you will find a range of light but appetising snacks such as Schinkenbrötchen or Käsebrötchen - simply ham or cheese sandwiches. Käseplatte is an enormous plate of cheese varieties, attractively garnished.

Evening meals (Abendessen) usually begin with soup. Popular are Kartoffelsuppe (potato soup), Gulaschsuppe (a meaty soup flavoured with paprika) or simply a Kraftbrühe (a clear soup) with either small dumplings, Nudeln (thin pasta) or Spätzle. The latter are very much a regional speciality and are a particularly delicious form of pasta, home-made, usually from wild wheat, eggy and light, and they are often served with the main course instead of potatoes. Should you wish to try an additional speciality, the Badische Schneckensuppe is a cream snail soup and quite delicious. Maultaschen are light square pockets of pastry filled with finely chopped meat, spinach and herbs and are another Baden speciality. They are equally good in soup or as a light meal when they are served in a cheese sauce. The fillings can of course vary. You sometimes are given a traditional starter at no cost whatsoever, comprising a small pot of good quality dripping (Schmalz) with some fresh bread, almost like a gesture of welcome as you wait for the first course you have ordered.

Pfifferlinge (chanterelles) are delicious little yellow mushrooms and are sometimes served as a dish in their own right which again is on the generous side. The many varieties of mushroom popular in Baden enhance the numerous dishes.

Locally caught trout are another speciality, served either natural (blau) or lightly fried with a dusting of flour (Müllerinart), usually with potatoes and a green salad. Meat dishes include Hirschragout (venison stew), Kalbsmedaillons (medallions of veal), Schweinschnitzel, pork steaks either fried in breadcrumbs, or with onions and mushrooms and a cream sauce, Ochsenfleisch with Meerenrettich (a popular dish of boiled beef with horseradish), Wildschwein (wild boar) and Wildentenbrust, an exquisite delicate dish of tender wild duck. Rice (Reis), potatoes or Spätzle are usually offered with these dishes and frequently a mixed salad is brought to you as a separate course to be eaten first. Geschnezeltes is another delicious dish, usually of strips of pork in a rich cream sauce with the customary accompaniments. Vegetables, normally varied and beautifully cooked, are served as an alternative to the salad. Vegetarian dishes are more limited in Germany, but most restaurants and larger Gasthäuser now offer some non-meat options, vegetable or cheese dishes and omelettes.

Sweet courses (Nachtisch or Dessert) usually consists of variations on the ice-cream, cream and fruit theme. This can be a variety of ices (Gemischtes Eis) which may include pistachio and walnut among several delicious varieties, or Kirschwasser Bomble which is a splendid confection of ice-cream, cream and cherries soaked in cherry schnapps.

Chocolate mousse or fresh fruit are also among the more usual offerings. Coffee and cake can be ordered for a welcome snack at almost any time and the famous Black Forest gâteau (Schwarzwalderkirschtorte) is in reality not the oversweet chocolate cake with a few cherries inside that pretends to that title outside Germany, but a splendid multi-layered cake with cherries soaked in Kirschwasser with alternate layers of cream, and can be dark or light in colour or a mixture of the two. A Preiselbeertorte is another delightful variation on the same theme. The Zwetschkenkuchen is again a regional speciality, fresh plums in a cake which is cut into large flattish squares; you are likely to be offered Sahne (cream) with it and it is highly recommended.

After a good day's walk it's nice to end the evening with a nightcap of one of the famous home-brewed Black Forest liqueurs. Amongst the most famous are Kirschwasser (cherry), Zwetschken (purple plum), Mirabelle (golden plum), Williams (pear), and Himbergeist (raspberry). If you find your way into the Renchtal, near Oberkirch, in the west of the Black Forest, you might even try the exotically named Topinambur (also called the Rossler), distilled from a tall plant introduced in the last century from South America as a means of clearing stretches of forest scrub and producing small yellow flowers and a form of potato used for horse and cattle feed.

The Official Black Forest Long Distance Routes

The three most famous high-level waymarked long distance routes through the Black Forest, the Westway, Middleway and Eastway, were all created between 1900 and 1903 and are almost certainly the earliest long distance waymarked trails in the world. They were the direct inspiration for the creation in 1917 of the Long Trail in the USA which runs from Massachusetts to the Canadian border, which led in turn to the creation of the famous Appalachian Trail, opened in 1937, and to Britain's first National Trail, the Pennine Way between Derbyshire and Scotland which was officially opened in 1965.

There are no less than eighteen officially recognised and waymarked long distance routes through the Black Forest, plus a series of specially designated Link Paths between the main routes, or between the main routes and important towns or villages.

The routes fall into four major categories. First are the three celebrated *Hohenwege* - the High-level Routes which run along the highest ridges of the Black Forest from north to south. Then follow the *Hauptwanderwege* - the Major Routes, most of them well established though not as long or as strenuous as the Hohenwege. Like the Hohenwege, they mainly run from north to south. The third category and just as important are the *Querwege* - the Traverse Routes which, as their name implies, cross the Black Forest in an east-west direction, intersecting with the other routes. Finally there are the *Zugangswege*, the Link Paths which take the walker to and from the main Hohenwege from the towns and larger villages, or act as linking routes between the Hohenwege.

Each of the different routes has its own coloured waymarked symbol to make clear to the walker which path to take. They are usually made of enamelled metal, though sometimes of cast iron or aluminium, or increasingly of vinyl to deter collectors. They are usually to be found nailed to trees but sometimes are on walls, telegraph poles, lamp posts or any convenient surface. These coloured diamonds are at times further enlivened by special markings; like a bunch of grapes in the wine growing regions or a rosehip for the Gäurandweg.

Apart from the official long distance walking routes recognised by the Black Forest Society, you may well find a variety of other symbols sharing a tree or a lamp post - sometimes a quite bewildering variety. Many of these are purely local routes, devised by local tourist offices as attractive circular walks from popular car parks, and have their own symbols - fir trees, fir cones, colours, letters, numbers, even a wild boar or a ladybird. You also find symbols, usually numerical, to denote cross-country ski routes. Others, like the attractive red and white clock face on the Clock Carriers' Way, are semi-official routes between hostels which often also utilise large sections of the official Black Forest Society's routes and Link Paths.

However attractive these waymarkings are, on no account be tempted to take them as souvenirs. Such irresponsible behaviour, when it does happen, can cause people considerable nuisance and delay, at worst serious risk of getting lost or injured. It is also theft. If you'd like such a souvenir, it is in fact possible to send off to the Schwarzwaldverein to purchase an original sign direct.

THE HOHENWEGE - HIGH-LEVEL ROUTES

1. The Westweg (Westway)

This is the first and oldest of the famous trio of Black Forest high-level routes which start at Pforzheim, an attractive market town on the northern fringe of the Black Forest famous for its jewellery museum. It ends at Basle in Switzerland. It is 281 km in length if you take the route over the Feldberg mountain (1,493m) or slightly longer at 285 km if you decide on a variation of the route over the Herzogenhorn. The route symbol is a red diamond on a white ground. Part of the route, from the Feldberg onwards, now forms part of the first European long distance footpath which stretches from the North Sea to Lake Constance, and over the St Gotthard Pass to the Mediterranean. The Westweg has some fairly steep sections where height is lost and regained to make it a fairly strenuous walk - it is often recommended as good training ground for mountain walking in the Alps.

The northern sections follow attractive paths mainly through woodland and there are some splendid panoramas as you wind your way up to the higher plateaux, taking in some of the highest mountains in the Black Forest (such as the Hornisgrinde (1,164m), the Feldberg (1,279m) and the Belchen (1,414m). Both route variations follow river valleys in the Basle direction and link together some important nature reserves.

2. The Mittelweg (Middleway)

This route, created in 1903, is 233 km in length and stretches from Pforzheim in the north to Waldshut in the south, forking at Lenzkirch with a choice of routes. Its symbol is a red diamond with a white flash, the whole on a white ground. It is known as the most romantic of the three Hohenwege because of its exceptionally beautiful scenery. It starts in mainly enclosed woodland in the north, following, for some distance, the old boundary between the states of Württemberg and Baden. From Schiltach onwards there are some splendid views, and the highest point of the walk is at Hochfirst (1,190m) near Neustadt, followed by the Stöcklewaldkopf (1,069m).

3. The Ostweg (Eastway)

The Ostweg is characterised as being the Hohenweg with most historic interest as it takes in numerous towers, ruins, and towns with interesting histories. It also starts at Pforzheim, and leads to Schaffhausen in the south. The latter has medieval buildings and was a well-known river port, for ships sailed up to this port on the River Rhine and then had their goods sent on by other means or unloaded and stored.

The route is 239 km in length and its symbol is a red and black diamond on a white ground. The paths cross fields and meadows far more frequently than the other routes, giving plenty of panoramic views. It is undeservedly less popular than the Westweg and the Mittelweg. A particular feature is the splendid beech woods which contrast with the darker conifers in the central region of the Black Forest. Perhaps its only disadvantage is that a number of main roads cross the route.

THE HAUPTWANDERWEGE (MAJOR ROUTES)

4. The Kandelhohenweg (Oberkirch - Freiburg)

The Kandelhohenweg is another very popular north-south route. It is 114 km in length and was created in 1935, its highly appropriate marking being a white 'K' on a red diamond on a white ground. At first the path follows the western section of the Black Forest to the foothills, then it crosses the River Elz and plunges once more into the forest till it reaches the highest peak of the central Black Forest, the Kandel mountain (1,243m). This route is heavily forested and is crossed by the Querweg Lahr-Rottweil and nearer Freiburg by the Gäurandweg.

5. The Rheinaue-Weg (Kehl - Basle)

The sign for this route which follows the banks of the River Rhine is again highly appropriate - blue waves in a white diamond on a white ground. A riverside and valley walk, it is 158 km in length and first runs close to the French and then the Swiss border, the river flowing below wine terraces in the north and west towards the more heavily wooded hills to the south. Kehl, originally a somewhat isolated fishing village, became important as a crossing point of the Rhine to Strasbourg, a city which throughout the centuries was alternately French or German according to boundary changes. Kehl is nowadays a particularly noted venue to eat freshly-grown asparagus when it is in season. There is a museum devoted to fishing and river boats in the town. Breisach, a mid-point on the route, is noted for its minster with a superb high-altar.

6. Gäurandweg (Mühlacker - Schopfloch)

99 km in length, the symbol of the Gäurandweg is a red rosehip on a green diamond on a white ground. The route follows an easterly direction through the Black Forest from the more sparsely populated Stroh and Heckengau areas to the more densely populated River Neckar region. Sections of moorland with juniper trees are a specially attractive feature. This route is particularly suitable for anyone who has not previously undertaken several days consecutive walking and would like to see how well they would cope. It is also recommended

for people with a particular interest in geology or botany.

7. Ortenauer Weinpfad - The Ortenauer Winepath (Baden-Baden to Offenburg)

This route was created in 1938 and is 63 km in length, starting at the sophisticated spa town of Baden-Baden and ending at the delightful historic wine town of Offenburg. Its symbol is a bunch of blue grapes in a red diamond on a white ground and it is a splendid walk through the steep terraces and vineyards above the Rhine Valley, much of it on level contours. There are variations in height as you climb between side valleys and up to various towers for panoramic views, then plunge back into the cooler woodlands. This is one of the few official Hauptwanderwege where a luggage carrying service is available.

8. Wii - Wegli (Staufen - Weil)

This route is 53 km in length and is sometimes called the Markgräfler Wiiwegle. Its symbol is a bunch of yellow grapes on a red diamond on a white ground. It runs across the extreme south-west corner of the Black Forest very near the Swiss border, another noted wine growing area. Staufen in the Breisgau is particularly associated with the Faust legend and the town still has a lot of medieval remains. Badenweiler which lies on the route is one of the oldest German spa towns whose thermal springs were first discovered by the Romans who founded the town in the first century. Sulzburg, a picturesque little town in the wine region, has a regional mining museum as silver and lead were mined in the area until 1832.

9. Kaiserstuhl Winzerweg - The Kaiserstuhl Wineway (Riegel - Achkarren)

This is a short route, only 16 km long, easily walked in a day. It is themed around vineyards and wine making and has a symbol consisting of blue grapes on a red diamond on a yellow ground. The soil around Kaiserstuhl is incredibly rich and volcanic and grows some exceptionally good wine. Its unusual shape led to the name of Emperor's Seat as the gouged out top looks like a huge and impressive armchair. The route includes some beautiful woodland and picturesque small wine growing towns and villages; Achkarren where the walk ends is one of these.

THE QUERWEGE (TRAVERSE ROUTES)

10. Querweg Gengenbach - Alpirsbach

This route is 51 km in length through central Schwarzwald, and is marked by a blue diamond on yellow ground. Gengenbach was an ancient free city with many interesting sights and was founded by the Zähringer dynasty. You climb 2,000 metres on this short Traverse Route and cross both the Westweg and the Mittelweg. This route is perhaps less popular because of its comparative steepness, though it is well worthwhile and is also good training for Alpine walking and for the feeling of being alone among the hills. Alpirsbach owes its origins to a Benedictine monastery and Gengenbach also has a monastic origin with interesting buildings dating from the thirteenth and fourteenth centuries and some baroque-style houses. Nowadays both towns are industrial though on a small scale. It has a continuation (same waymark) as the Kaiserstuhl Nord-Sud Weg (North-South Way).

11. Querweg Lahr - Rottweil

This route is 93 km in length and runs through the heart of the Black Forest. It has a red and blue diamond on a yellow ground as its waymark symbol. It provides a useful east-west link with several other popular routes such as the Kandelhohenweg, Westweg, Mittelweg and the Ostweg. Lahr, in the Rhine Valley was originally settled by the Romans and the various archaeological finds can be seen in the local museum. Interesting architectural features abound from the twelfth to the nineteenth centuries in such towns passed on the route as Hornberg, Königsfeld as well as Rottweil itself, and the route takes in some particularly fine forest walking.

Buchberg with its 1,000-year old church of St Nikolaus is particularly worth a visit as is Rottweil, a former fortified town with a number of places of interest. The town also gave its name to the breed of dogs who were bred to guard the cattle in earlier times from attacks by wolves.

12. Querweg Schwarzwald-Jura-Bodensee (St Georgen - Radolfzell)
This route was created in 1935 and is 109 km in length, starting in St Georgen and ending in Radolfzell on the Bodensee. Its symbol is a green diamond on a yellow ground. The area round St Georgen is part of the great clock making centre. Villingen, another old walled Zähringer market town is very picturesque. Bad Dürrheim is a spa with the site of the highest brine bath in Europe. The opening of the Bodensee autobahn has perhaps spoilt the section of route between Villingen-Offingen, but parts of the Ostweg can be used instead for this section. The route goes south towards the Bodensee, crosses the Hengau and, on the stretch between Engen and Singen, shares the way with the Querweg Freiburg-Bodensee.

13. Querweg Kaiserstuhl-Rhein (Donaueschingen - Breisach)
This route is 110 km long and is marked by a red diamond on yellow ground. Donaueschingen has a splendid stately home, the Seat of the Lords of Fürstenberg with the Danube fountain in the grounds. Furtwangen in upper Bregtal is the home of an outstanding collection of Black Forest clocks which forms part of the German National Clock Museum. Waldkirch in Elztal is a small town at the foot of the Kandel massif overlooked by Kastelburg and has much of interest. On this walk you go from the Baar plateau and reach the Rhine-Danube watershed at Neueck with comparatively little climbing. The woodland route then leads into the Gutach Valley and later the Elz Valley and between the Forest and the Kaiserstuhl mountain for about 15 km over the Rhine plateau. The last section follows the northern edge of the Kaiserstuhl hills and heads on to Breisach with ever-varying scenery.

14. Schwarzwald Nordrandweg (Mühlacker - Pforzheim - Karlsruhe)
The Nordrandweg is a 67 km route which runs along the northern edge of the Black Forest, starting at Mühlacker and forming a link from the Gäurandweg to Pforzheim before turning northwards to the city of Karlsruhe. Its waymark is a white diamond on a yellow ground.

15. Querweg Freiburg-Bodensee

This is perhaps the most famous and finest of all the traverse routes, often named with the three Hohenwege as Schwarzwald's Big Four. It starts from the beautiful city of Freiburg in the south-west of the Black Forest, with its splendid cathedral, bustling market square, old town gateways and wealth of architectural interest, and runs to the Bodensee (Lake Constance). The route is 178 km long and its symbol is a white and red diamond on a yellow ground. It is perhaps the most spectacular route of all in terms of the variety and dramatic nature of the scenery, and it also carries part of the first European long distance footpath en route to the Mediterranean. It is particularly noteworthy for the dramatic gorges through which it runs, such as the Ravennaschlucht and the celebrated Wutachschlucht (a valley which has had to be saved several times from industrial developments). Konstanz, where the walk ends, is a charming old city in a beautiful lake setting, formerly ruled by bishops. The Bodensee is shared by Austria, Germany and Switzerland whose boundaries all converge here. It is the warmest area in Germany and enjoys a climate famed for fruit and vegetable growing.

16. Hotzenwald-Querweg (Schopfheim - Waldshut)

This 45 km route has a white and black diamond on yellow ground and runs through the hills in the southern Black Forest close to the Swiss border. From Schopfheim the route skirts the edge of the Dinkel mountains, then there is a steep climb up to the Hotzenwald Becken (1,028m) with splendid views. It is worth remembering that the Germans often refer to the Swiss as the *Eidgenossen* (those who have sworn an oath - in other words, Republicans). It is no coincidence that so close to this border there was an uprising of a group of rebels known as the Salpeteres during the eighteenth century, which continued over a long period and was only suppressed with difficulty. The Hotzenwald has a number of hydro-electric power stations. Many of the small towns on this route are renowned for their bracing climate.

17. Hansjakobweg

This route has an intriguing black hat on a white diamond on white ground for a symbol. Heinrich Hansjakob was a nineteenth century parson and much loved Black Forest writer who was frequently to be seen wearing a black, broad-brimmed hat or *Schlapphut*. The longer circular route starts at Haslach, his birthplace, and goes through Wolfach with its museum of carnival masks, then on to Brandenkopf, and finally to Zell and Höhenhauser before returning to Haslach. This route is 106 km in length; the shorter circular route, about 51 km in length, starts and ends at the village of Schapbach Dorf.

18. Hochrein Querweg (Rheinfelden - Albbruck)

This 49 km-long route was founded in 1941 and runs along the southern part of the Black Forest through Wehr and Egg, along the hills overlooking the Rhine Valley. It has a white and blue diamond on a yellow ground as a waymark. A number of alterations have taken place in recent years, so make sure you use an up-to-date map if you plan to walk the route. There are good views from several points into the Upper Rhine Valley and the Wieladingen ruins passed in the forest nearby are an interesting feature.

ZUGANGSWEGE (LINK PATHS)

19. Zugangswege zum Westweg vom Rheintal

Marked by a blue diamond on white ground, this path provides a useful linking route from the Rhine Valley to the Westweg.

20. Zugangs und Verbindungswege Zwischen den Hohenwegen

A whole series of paths indicated by a blue diamond with white flash on white ground. These provide well marked and very useful connecting links between the three Hohenwege themselves or directly to or from towns and larger villages in the Black Forest and the Hohenwege.

21. Zugangswegen zum Ostweg von Neckar

This is a yellow and blue diamond on white ground and is used on link routes from the Neckar Valley, east of the Schwarzwald, to the Ostweg.

Grapes - Ortenauer Winepath
Baden-Baden

Theatre, Baden-Baden. The start of the Ortenauer Winepath.

Vineyards and view of Rhine Valley above Bühl (Day 1, Winepath).

Black Forest Walking Routes with Point-to-Point Luggage Transfer
These routes are largely walks which take in sections of official Black Forest Society routes but are marketed, usually by the local tourist office in the area, as walking holidays using local guest-houses, hotels or inns. The pre-arranged accommodation is generally of very good quality and the landlords arrange to have your luggage transported to the next overnight stop. The all-in price usually includes overnight accommodation, bed and breakfast or half-board (check what package you are getting), and luggage transfer.

All the routes shown below are officially recognised by the Baden-Württemburg State Tourist Office who issue a brochure each year giving up-to-date information. It can be obtained free of charge from the German National Tourist Offices in the UK, or USA and most other countries, or from the Fremdenverkehrsverband Schwarzwald e.V., Bertoldstraße 45, Postfach 1660, 7800 Freiburg im Breisgau, Germany.

With one exception (Spätzlespfaden) they are self-guided walks, and though detailed route descriptions are available when you book the package, they are usually in German. Tracing the route out on the map even with shaky German is not likely to be a problem for experienced walkers, and you will almost invariably meet travelling companions to share your journey over one or more days. There is no nicer way of making new friends than to discuss the finer points of route finding in German, English or a combination of the two.

But to make life easier, in Part Three of this book we have taken two very fine examples of *öhne Gepäck* walking packages which are bookable direct from the UK or USA - the Ortenauer Winepath and the Clock Carriers' Way - and given very much more detailed description in the text than is otherwise available in English. We have done this because we believe that for most people from outside Germany this is by far the easiest way of enjoying some of the finest walking the Black Forest has on offer.

For further details and information, including booking arrangements, for each of these walking holidays, write to the addresses given on the following pages.

1. Along the Tracks of the Red Deer

This route starts at Freudenstadt, a town in the northern Black Forest extensively restored after war damage and with a magnificent central square. The waymarking for the walk is a green deer on a white ground and the route can last up to ten days. At several points of the walk you are likely to see the herds of red deer. You actually cross sections of the Westweg and Mittelweg (High-level Routes) on the walk and take in the Bühlerhöhekurhaus, an area famous for its plum growing and for the dramatic story of the Bühlerhöhe. This was originally built as a convalescent home for officers by a wealthy heiress who hoped to gain an entrée into society, but whose Jewish ancestry, divorce and remarriage gave ample rein to prejudice. The lady, who was disappointed both in her ambitions and in her love, eventually committed suicide, but ironically the stylish building later became a very exclusive *Kurhotel* for the rich and famous who made use of the sanatorium facilities she had had built in the grounds.

You finish the walk at Kniebis, if you complete the whole route, from where it is easy to return to Freudenstadt.

Details and booking: Kurverwaltung Freudenstadt, Postfach 440, 7290 Freudenstadt, Germany.

2. The Clock Carriers' Way

This delightful route runs through areas of the Black Forest particularly linked with clock making, and takes in such spectacular features as the Brend and Hochfirst peaks, and the Gutachtal and Wutachtal gorges in the central area of the Black Forest. Excellent high quality hotels are used throughout on a half-board package. It makes a first class introduction to typical scenery of the Black Forest and is described in much greater detail in Part Three of this book.

Details and booking: Kurverwaltung, 7740 Triberg im Schwarzwald, Germany; or Parkhotel Wehrle, D-7740 Triberg im Schwarzwald, Germany. A coloured brochure about the walk is available in English.

3. The Feldberg Circular

This route in the southern Black Forest around the Feldberg mountain is about 160 km long and each stage of the route varies from between 10 to 20 km. The route (waymarked with a green and white medallion of fir trees, walkers and the Feldberg tower) starts at the Titisee, one of the loveliest natural lakes in the Black Forest, and goes over Hinterzarten up to the Feldberg mountain (1,500m), the highest mountain in the region. From here it continues to the spa town of Notschrei, whose name recalls the pressing need for a road from the Wiesental to Freiburg. When it was finally brought about in 1848 the Emergency Call, as the town is named, had been heeded.

You next climb up the heights of the Belchen mountain and head on to the beautiful Wiesental where there are some splendid waterfalls. Toodmoos-Strick is so-called because the horses used to be changed here in the olden days and the others ready for hire were generally bound together with a rope or *Strick*. You later go through the area which has achieved fame through the television series *Black Forest Clinic* and pass the house of the hero, Professor Brinkmann. You return to the Titisee after covering a route filled with historic farmhouses, old mills and Black Forest legends.

Details and booking: Kurverwaltung, 7820 Titisee-Neustadt, Germany.

4. The Spätzle Paths

This is a 7-day walk in the north of the Black Forest which can be done only on a given series of dates between the end of April and the end of May, and from mid-September until late October. It starts and finishes at Bad Herrenalb, taking in a number of charming spa resorts, and is walked as an official group with a leader - a nice opportunity to meet other people. (Spätzle are a lovely light form of pasta, one of the delightful regional specialities of the Black Forest.)

Details and booking: Herrenalber Reisebüro, In Stadthaus, 7560 Bad Herrenalb, Germany.

5. Along the Murgtal Way

The Murg Valley runs southwards from Baden-Baden and is famed for its gigantic conifers which used to be made into rafts and floated down the river. It is a 5-day walk, each day covering distances between 17 and 23 km, which takes place any time between April and November. It starts and finishes at the village of Gernsbach near Baden-Baden.

Details and booking: Verkehrsamt Gernsbach, Igelbachstraße 11, 7562 Gernsbach, Germany.

6. The Ortenauer Winepath

This is the only one of the Schwarzwald Major Routes which has a specific walking package along it. It uses a route which goes between vineyards and forests on the sunny western slopes of the Black Forest above the Rhine Valley. It can last from three to six days - full details in Part Three.

Details and booking: Verkehrsamt Offenburg, Gärtenstraße 6, 7600 Offenburg, Germany.

7. The Black Forest Water-mill Tour

A 5-day walking tour in the central Black Forest taking in a number of old water-mills and linking up four attractive villages in the Acher and Sasbach valleys. Easy walking, each day covering between 10-14 km.

Details and booking: Kurverwaltung, Postfach 1108, 7595 Sasbachwalden, Germany.

8. Schwarzwald-Baar and Wutach Rambling Weeks

A week of walking in some of the most picturesque countryside in the central and southern Black Forest, starting and finishing in Donaueschingen. One special feature is a day spent on the Wutachbahn - the Wutach steam railway that runs from Zollhaus-Blumberg to Weizen (see Part One).

Details and booking: Stadt Verkehrsamt, Karlstraße 58, 7710 Donaueschingen, Germany.

9. The Black Forest Wutach Gorge Circular

A week's walking with some longish days (up to 29 km) taking in the whole of the spectacular Wutachschlucht and utilising several stretches of Hohenweg or Querweg.

Details and booking: Verkehrsamt Villingen-Schwenningen, Romäusring 2, 7730 Villingen-Schwenningen, Germany.

PART THREE

The Ortenauer Winepath

Baden-Baden to Offenburg through Vineyard and Forest

The Ortenauer Winepath is one of the shortest of the Black Forest Society's Major Routes and can easily be fitted into three or four days of a Black Forest holiday. Alternatively the walk can be extended for an additional two days from Zell-Weierbach to Gengenbach and Diersburg.

The Wine Path, established in 1938, is largely a contour route, following the western flanks of the Black Forest overlooking the Rhine Valley. Much of it is on vineyard tracks or forest paths through the outskirts of Baden-Baden and Bühl and the Ortenauer, the wine growing region which has Offenburg as its capital and gives its name to the route.

This is not difficult walking county; much of it is on fairly level, stony or even tarmac paths along terraces between vineyards, though with some steady climbing out of the side valleys which drain the central massif. The waymark is an attractive bunch of blue grapes set in a red diamond, and generally the route is extremely well waymarked (on trees and on vinestands). However, in late summer leaves can obscure the diamond and you sometimes have to look carefully to find it.

Unlike most of the Black Forest Major Routes the Ortenauer Winepath is also marketed as a pre-bookable *öhne Gepäck* (without luggage) package between comfortable small hotels and inns, with luggage transfers arranged at a cost of only 5Dm (just under £2) per person per night, payable at the previous night's accommodation.

For full details (including information about an optional wine seminar and booking) write in English or German, to Stadt Offenburg Kultur und Verkehrsamt, Gärtnerstraße 6, 7600 Offenburg. Alternatively a direct booking of travel and accommodation for whatever combination you choose can be made within the UK

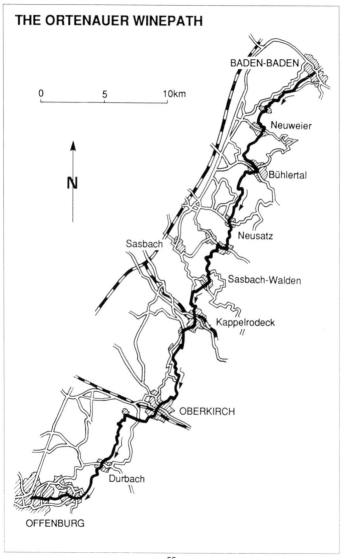

THE ORTENAUER WINEPATH

through DER Travel Service, 18 Conduit Street, London W1 (Tel: 071 486 4593).

Because so much of this route goes through vineyards which are normally close to the public during grape ripening and harvest time (August to early October), special permission is given to walkers on the Ortenauer Winepath in the form of a permit available from the tourist office (address above) in return for an undertaking from the leader of the party that no grapes will be eaten during the walk! But, as more than adequate compensation, it is usually possible each evening of the walk to drink the wine from the grapes of the vineyards through which you have passed in the form of excellent Qualitäts wine in open carafe at an extremely reasonable price.

Should you walk the Ortenauer Winepath during grape ripening time, you may hear what seems to be repeated gunshots across the vineyards. These are produced by simple mechanical devices to scare the birds away from the grapes and do not threaten your safety. You will also notice at times along the Ortenauer Winepath old wine presses, darkened with age and spilling over with flowers, a reminder of ancient wine making processes.

The main Baden-Baden to Offenburg section (64 km) can be done by experienced walkers in three days. The going is fairly easy throughout, though the second day (23 km) is fairly long and many people may prefer to split it, perhaps stopping overnight at Kappelrodeck or Waldulm, making two very easy days. What we would very strongly recommend, however, is that you arrange your visit to give adequate time - at least half a day in both cases and preferably a full day - to exploring the lovely old towns of Baden-Baden and Offenburg, at the beginning and at the end of your walk. Both are enchanting in quite different ways.

The recommended map for the whole of the Ortenauer Winepath is the Schwarzwaldverein/LBW 1:50,000, Sheet 2 Baden-Baden Hornisgrinde.

DAY ONE - BADEN-BADEN TO NEUSATZ
Distance: 22 km   Time: 6¹/₂ hours

Baden-Baden is a spa town of considerable elegance - a combination of Harrogate, Cheltenham and Bath with much more besides - in a gracious setting. There are ancient Roman baths, hospitals to cure various rheumatic conditions, a sparkling new swimming pool and saunas, Caracalla-Therme themed in Roman-style, special Roman-Irish (actually more like Turkish) baths, a Trinkalle where you can taste the warm springs, a bandstand where the spa orchestra plays Strauss and Lehar, a casino, gardens, lawns, fountains, sophisticated shops, boutiques and parades. Narrow streets have an almost Mediterranean feel about them with balconies dripping flowers and pots of colourful oleanders on the pavement. There is an excellent choice of hotels and restaurants.

As a fashionable spa Baden-Baden was almost discovered by accident by some bored diplomats at nearby Rastatt, in the time of the French Emperor Napoleon, who sought distraction from the interminable wrangling over treaties. A few miles away was this rather charming place with excellent food and apparently cheap champagne. Baden-Baden became in due course a mecca for all the crowned heads of Europe as well as for anyone with any pretensions to the fashionable world.

If you arrive by train, the station on the main line to Basle is about 4 km from the town centre and with luggage it's much easier to take a taxi or wait for one of the fairly frequent buses into town.

The Winepath begins at the right-hand side of the elegant theatre, close to the casino and bandstand in the town centre. Follow Werderstrasse, a tree-lined road with elegant villas. After around 200m fork left into Beutingweg - you should see your first grape waymark on the 'No Through Road' sign. This is a steep, narrow lane which soon climbs to join the main road again, now called Moltkerstraße, at a crossroads.

Climb ahead along Moltkerstraße but look for a path into the wood on the right, waymarked and marked with a stone - the Kaiserin Augusta Weg. This woodland path runs parallel to the main road past a memorial stone to Empress Augusta. At the next crossroads

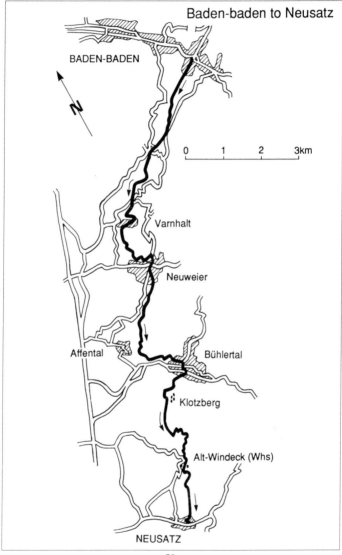

Baden-baden to Neusatz

keep ahead, the path now lower than the main road, above a wooded ravine.

You eventually emerge at the Tiergarten bus-stop near traffic lights. Keep along the main road in the same direction, crossing the road to pass a golf course on the left and then the Fairway Hotel complex. Soon, past the hotel, bear left up a forest track which ascends to the road by the Entenstall Hütte bus-stop. Keep left along the road for a few metres before bearing left down another forest track where the notice 'Schranke!' warns of a vehicle barrier. This path descends through the forest into Grünbachtal.

For the first time you sense you are in the real Black Forest as you go deep into woodland by massive fir trees. At the fish farm, bear left between the ponds before ascending to join a gravel track which climbs through the forest to emerge at a little wooden shelter, grillplatz (barbecue) and spring - the Hütte am Nellele - at the edge of the vineyards.

Outside the grillplatz is the first of several stone plaques, it explains the history of this particular vineyard which dates back to the ninth century and expanded in monastic times. Types of grape and the percentage of each variety grown here are also detailed - Riesling 60%, Sylvaner 30% and Müller Thurgau 10%.

From the plaque turn left for a few metres along the lane before going right (look for waymarks) along a high-level tarmac wine track through the mature vineyards. There you find the first of several magnificent views you will enjoy on the route across the vineyards and into the Rhine Valley. The track - only walkers along the Winepath are allowed through here - climbs to a beautiful modern chapel (Josefs Kapelle) decorated with flowers, a delightful viewpoint.

One of the delights of the Ortenauer Winepath is finding various little chapels along the route - some in baroque-style, others modern where wood and stone are often imaginatively used. All offer cool shade - and place for spiritual reflection - on a hot day.

Continue along the track, turning left at the junction curving along Klosterbergstraße into the top end of the village of Varnhalt, at Oberdorf. It's worth going into the village centre for morning coffee at the Gasthof. Otherwise bear left along the Kastanienhalde. At a fork keep right, this time signed to Yburg; keep ahead at the next junction once again into the vineyards. There are fine views across to Steinbach and the Rhine Valley, the scarlet pantiled roofs contrasting against the vivid greens of the vines. Keep to the main path but when you reach a crossroads bear right. Continue ahead at the next junction. The main track contours along the hillside, soon bearing left. Keep left at a memorial cross, the way swinging into a side valley before curving towards the village of Neuweier. Like Varnhalt, Neuweier together with the villages of Umweg and Steinbach, are permitted to sell their wines in the characteristic flask-like Bocksbeutel-shape. Neuweier also has a speciality wine known as Mauerwein. Fork left at a house with an appropriate mural of a Bocksbeutel, and descend the equally apt Bocksbeutelstraße into the town.

Gasthaus zum Traube, near the church, makes a useful lunch stop. The Winepath continues across the road and along the well named Weinstraße, ascending past the school and Gasthaus zum Alder Gott before taking the road forking left, Losenbergstraße, which soon bears right. As the houses end the Winepath turns into Heiligenstraße, but soon turns sharp right back into the vineyards which in late summer and autumn are richly coloured by red grape vines, the leaves as vivid as the fruit. The track is now parallel with and above the road along the Eisental Valley, again with splendid views. Keep ahead now on the main path (check the waymarks!) for about a kilometre to a T-junction at a tarmac road above a picnic place. Cross over to locate a narrow path into the wood which leads to a little chapel on the left - Mariebrunnen - with a spring and rest area. Keep left at the next junction, soon reaching another viewpoint and grillplatz by a spring, Heissersteinbrunnen.

From here the Winepath follows the Panorama Way, a section of path with quite splendid views across the Affental, famous for its rich red wines which were introduced by the Cistercian monastery of Lichental here in the twelfth century. The word 'Affen' means 'monkeys' and 'tal' is 'valley,' but in fact the strange name is really a corruption of something quite different. The story goes that a chapel once stood in the area whose bell called the faithful to prayers, the Ave Maria. This became corrupted in time to 'Ave-Tal,' then to 'Afental' and eventually 'Affental.'

The way curves left above Altschweir village and into the Bühler Valley. At a three-way crossroads yours is the middle path which leads directly into the valley. Look at waymarks to confirm your route (other landscape features are difficult to find) but if you take the wrong track do not worry, all rejoin on the descent into Bühlertal. The correct route will lead to a T-junction where you turn left into Sessgaße, following it past a crossroads to reach a path by a house on the right, going down steps into the centre of the village with its handsome parish church.

The route continues past the church and across the main road at traffic lights, taking the underpass then turning left along the main road before going right into Matthäuserstraße. Look for a track right, this turns by gardens and soon becomes a lovely grassy way past small vineyards, then joins the road. After about 30m the way turns right down a narrow lane signed 'Im Kössler' - fine views again here. At a junction the route is left, then first right, curving deep into a wood. Look out left for a narrow path through the woods (waymarked) which climbs to a track. Turn right past a farmhouse and head back into the wood. The way re-emerges in vineyards. At a crossroads turn left uphill, up steps. Keep ahead along the path marked to Burg Alt Windeck which narrows through handsome chestnut and beech trees before emerging at a bend. Turn left here back into vines, but look for yet another narrow, even steeper path which climbs through young woodland. This reaches a forest track. Turn right here.

At a 200-year-old tree - a plaque explains its age - the way forks to the left, climbing to Burg Alt Windeck, a fortified tower at the height of its importance in the thirteenth and early fourteenth centuries, now a celebrated restaurant. You emerge by a car park area. The Winepath continues past the entrance to the Burg and is soon a lovely forest path through tall pines. This well-marked path descends sharply but steadily before joining a farm road and lane into Neusatz. Turn left past the fire station to find a path that leads into the village.

Neusatz is a typical, small Black Forest town of charm and character, totally unspoiled by tourism, quietly getting on with its worldly business but welcoming those visitors - usually on foot - that find their way there. There is a handsome little church, a couple of excellent Gasthäuser, a main street of attractive but unpretentious houses and a fine setting of forest and vineyards. What more could a tired walker desire?

DAY TWO - NEUSATZ TO OBERKIRCH
Distance: 23 km   Time: 7 hours

From the Gasthof zum Linde in the centre of Neusatz take the lane opposite but slightly to the right - Bittersteg - which soon becomes a steep and stony track with a handrail, climbing past orchards. You reach the pretty hamlet of Gebersberg. Turn right, along Geberstraße, keeping straight ahead at the crossroads. This quiet, level lane, relaxing after the climb from Neusatz, takes you past little farms, orchards, gardens, pasture and small woods. After about 2 km you descend into Laufbachtal to the hamlet of Auf. Turn right into the main road, but after 150m turn left into Neu Windeckstraße, soon climbing past an old farm, Matzenhof. Keep ahead at the crossroads, the lane gradually climbing out of the valley and turning upwards to Neu Windeck - despite its name another ruined medieval tower, also a fine viewpoint across to Ottersweir and beyond.

The way follows the lane left past farms, keeping ahead at the crossroads and next junction through the hamlet of Grimmes Haus where you'll find a house with a variety of clocks, ornaments and mottos (including a reference to the Ortenauer Winepath). Now the route becomes a gravel path through vineyards, with views across to Sasbach and its monastery. Follow the way as it descends to Kammerhof, a handsome farm. Turn right at the farm and follow the farm track as it curves around left, keeping left at the next junction and at the next fork where the Winepath takes the higher and broader lane through extensive terraces of vines, with fine views across the valley. Fork right at the next junction, past a little shrine and bench.

This shrine is dedicated to the story of Alder Gott which relates to the Thirty Years War and the tremendous devastation and loss of life it caused in the seventeenth century. Apparently there were no inhabitants left in one village in the area as a young man came by thinking sadly that he would never find a wife. At that moment he spotted a young woman who had survived. Overjoyed he made her acquaintance, they married and planted their first vine at the exact spot where they first met, then planted further vines and raised a family. The exclamation 'Alde Gotte!' ('Thanks be to God!') was the cry of joy made by the delighted young man when he

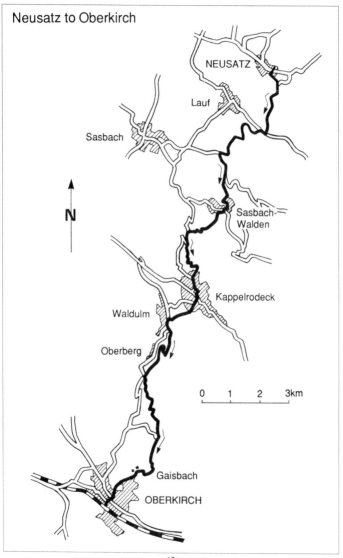

Neusatz to Oberkirch

NEUSATZ

Lauf

Sasbach

N

Sasbach-
Walden

Kappelrodeck

Waldulm

Oberberg

0   1   2   3km

Gaisbach

OBERKIRCH

Traditional houses, Oberkirch

discovered his future wife.

Keep on the lane to reach the outlying houses of Sasbachwalden. Keep on the broader road downhill into the centre of this little health resort, with attractive black and white houses complete with a genuine Black Forest health clinic and choice of guest-houses and inns.

Turn left at the junction past Gasthaus Gaishöll, then sharp right along a narrow path across meadowland to a footbridge, going right then left then right, zig-zagging uphill. Waymarks avoid confusion. The route joins a tarmac track curving uphill signed 'Auf der Ecke.' Just past the summit fork right, this time towards Kappelrodeck Kapelle, through more vineyards and past a large, handsome farmhouse.

Rodeck is in fact a twelfth century look-out tower. Kappelrodeck is also famous for the Witch of Dasenstein, the name of a large granite rock which dominates the scene and also the name of an excellent local red wine (Die Hex von Dasenstein). Furthermore this same character plays a prominent role in the Shrovetide carnival celebrations known as Fastnacht.

Westway
Pforzheim — Basle

Middleway
Pforzheim — Waldshut

Eastway
Pforzheim-Schaffhausen

Kandel-High Level Route
Oberkirch-Freiburg

Rheinaue-way
Kehl-Basel

Gäurand-way
Mühlacker-Schopfloch

Ortenauer Winepath
Baden-Baden - Offenburg

Wii-Wegli
Staufen-Weil

Kaiserstuhl Wine Way
Riegel-Achkarren

Traverse Route
Gengenbach-Alpirsbach
and Kaiserstühl NS Way

Traverse Route
Lahr-Rottweil

Schwarzwald-Jura-
Bodensee
(Lake Constance) Way
St Georgen-Radolfzell

Traverse Route
Donaueschingen-Breisach

Schwarzwald- North Way
Mühlacker-Pforzheim-
Karlsruhe

Traverse Route
Freiburg-Bodensee
(Lake Constance)

Hotzenwald Traverse Route
Schopfheim-Waldshut

Hansjakob Way

Hochrhein Traverse Route
Rheinfelden-Albbruck

Link Path to the Westway
from the Rhine Valley

Link Paths for the
High-Level Routes

Link Paths to the Eastway
from the Neckar Area

Waymarks in the Black Forest

Vineyards and forest near Neusatz (Day 1, Ortenauer Winepath)

Flowers in basket, Matzen (Day 2, Ortenauer Winepath)

The Winepath swings to the right, a sandy track by the vines. At the main road follow the path sharp left back into the wood, parallel and above the road - there are lovely views of the Achental Valley. The path joins a broader track, back into the vines, and is a particularly lovely and scenic stretch of route which finally dips into the edge of the town of Kappelrodeck. Gasthof Adler, on the left as you reach the main road in town, is well placed to serve the needs of walkers.

Kappelrodeck itself is an interesting small town. You pass a large paper factory as you walk into town, and on the right as you cross the bridge is one of the numerous small private distilleries in the Black Forest that produce such schnapps as Kirsch and Williams. But the Ortenauer Winepath turns left before reaching the distillery, going down Herrenmatte by a wood yard and cottages to a level-crossing by Kappelrodeck station, now operated by the regional transport authority as a local line. Museum trains are operated by steam locomotives on summer Sundays between Achern and Ottenhöfen.

Cross the tracks, but keep left at the level-crossing along the line before going right into the town centre - again with a good choice of restaurants and accommodation. The route goes up Waldamarstraße, as it bends keep ahead up Jahnstraße following the signs to Achertal Sporthalle, which you soon pass. The road climbs steeply - keep ahead towards Waldulm, along Echäldele past pleasant suburban houses. At a crossroads the way narrows to become a traffic-free path, lined with birch and chestnut, into Waldulm (yet another place noted for its red wine).

Turn left along the main road through Waldulm, a scattered settlement with several places for refreshment. Where the main road swings to the right the Winepath follows a lane along the valley floor beside the Fautenbach stream.

Where the road bends left the Winepath goes directly ahead up a steep track, past a farm and back into the vineyards. The route now climbs and curves sharply round in a U-bend, with fine views back down the valley. Keep on the main, higher path as it swings left, going sharp left at a fork. Where the vines end, near a 1744 shrine, the path continues ahead into woods to eventually reach a road at the Gasthaus zum Einkehr.

Turn left here under a stone bridge but almost immediately take the way which branches off left under pylons, back into the woods. Keep left, following the waymarks, the track now climbing above vineyards and around the edge of the wood. You soon reach an attractive shelter - the Walkers' Rest - and a superb viewpoint across the enclosed valley above Oberkirch, an area of lovely cherry orchards above Ringelbach. At the T-junction turn left, curving back into the wood and past crags, with some magnificent mature trees - mainly beech and firs. At the next T-junction the way is right, still through woods, but soon climbing to the left to the Fellhäuserhütte Waldparkplatz (forest parking place) with its wooden hut and benches.

From the hut the Winepath curves back off the main track along a forest path to the right which zig-zags sharply down to yet another little ruined castle in the forest, the Ruine Schausenberg, an impressive structure of outer walls, gateways and a tall keep. It is open for visitors to wander around - at your own risk! Again there are impressive views into the main Renchtal Valley.

You may find some rather tall plants growing in the fields here, instead of vines, with large narrow leaves and bright yellow flowers like a large marguerite. These are called Topinambur and have an interesting history. They were originally imported from South America and have a root crop not unlike the potato. However, it was found that this was totally unsuitable for human beings, but could be used for horses and therefore became known as Roßäpfel (Roß is the colloquial name for horse). Later still the Topinambur was made into a strong schnapps, called Rossler, which is known virtually only in the Renchtal and can be tasted at some of the local inns. The Topinambur plants were found to be very useful when clearing the ground, since their height and density inhibited the growth of smaller plants around them.

The Renchtal also boasts a famous son, Hans Jakob Christoff von Grimmelshausen who lived during the period of the Thirty Years War and wrote a famous satirical account of those times with an anti-hero called Simplicius Simplicissimus. He later went on to become mayor of nearby Renchen. The celebrated twentieth century dramatist, Bertolt Brecht, based his character of Mother Courage (who follows that same war with her baggage wagon, trying to eke out a precarious living) on the figure of Courasche from these earlier writings. Grimmelshausen married at Oberkirch and his own life was almost as adventurous as that of the famous Simplicius.

The route to Oberkirch leaves from the western side of the castle and is a narrow path around the perimeter fence of a lodge, steeply zig-zagging down through vegetation. It eventually becomes a farm track leading into the hamlet of Gaisbach.

Keep ahead for over a kilometre to the main crossroads where if you turn left you'll come to the centre of the lovely little seventeenth century town of Oberkirch.

Oberkirch is in fact the fruit growing centre of the Ortenau with the largest strawberry market in the whole of Germany. The origins of its wine industry date back to the eleventh century. It has a busy town centre, a fine church and carefully preserved half-timbered merchants' and butchers' houses grouped around the rapidly flowing Rench river.

DAY THREE - OBERKIRCH TO OFFENBURG
Distance: 17 km   Time: 5 hours

Make your way through Oberkirch's old town centre to the railway station, going over the railway at the level-crossing and continuing along Obersdorfstraße to the bridge over the canalised section of the River Rench (built to eliminate flood risk at times of snow melt).

The Winepath follows the southern bank of the river, downstream, past the next bridge. Turn left at a little building to cross the edge of a park and sports field, veering left to join along Butschbaker Straße. Keep ahead past a single block of flats, and at a crossroads take the road signed 'Am Eckenberg.' The road soon begins to climb sharply, curving to the right by a wayside cross, passing old farms and barns.

Where the road bends left the Winepath bears off right, by another cross, down a grassy track. Note a sad memorial plaque marking the spot where three soldiers were killed in April 1945, a matter of weeks before the ceasefire that ended the Second World War.

Follow what now becomes a farm track, sweeping past a farm. Look for a narrow fieldpath (left) that cuts off the corner as the track bends and heads for a crossroads by tall cypresses. Take the lane opposite, St Wendelstraße, which climbs past a large farmhouse, Froschof, and open fields. The lane edges around the village of

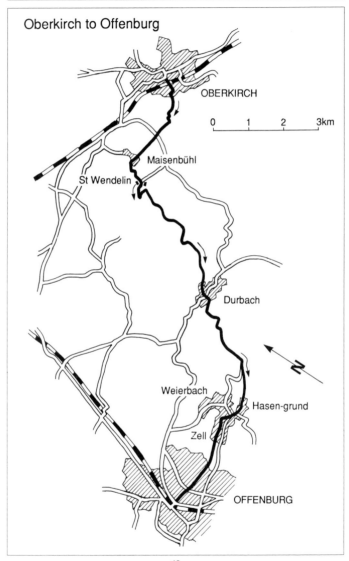

Oberkirch to Offenburg

OBERKIRCH

0   1   2   3km

Maisenbühl

St Wendelin

Durbach

N

Weierbach

Hasen-grund

Zell

OFFENBURG

Maisenbühl with its suburban houses, but there are good views into the Weidenbach Valley. Continue gently upwards, turning left at the crossroads, past chestnut trees and past fields of fruit and arable crops including, possibly, the remarkable Topinambur plant still grown in the Renchtal district to make strong schnapps.

The little 18th century chapel of St Wendel is well worth a visit. It is beautifully situated on the edge of the forest with benches for walkers and a grotto nearby.

The route now enters the forest to the right of the chapel, following a track which emerges at another hut and rest place this time at Minster View - the minster in question (visible if it is a clear day) being Strasbourg cathedral, across the Rhine and in France.

You are now back in the vineyards. The Winepath hairpins sharp left uphill above the forest then winds up to a tiny summit chapel in the middle of the vines, again a fine viewpoint. Continue on what is now a stony path along a low ridge through landscape of great beauty. Keep ahead at the first crossroads but bear left, with waymarks, at the next junction of tracks, climbing steeply to another little shrine and viewpoint in the vines.

Keep ahead to where the path forks by a little shelter. The way is to the right and curves along the edge of a wood. At the next junction keep left and maintain your height along the track marked Schloss Staufenberg. (Note: the waymarks differ from the route as shown on the map - follow the waymarks.) When you arrive at a farm follow the track to the left of the huge old tree, which climbs around the side of the castle to the entrance.

The original castle here was the scene of the medieval legend of Melusine. Long ago a knight, Peter von Staufenberg, fell in love with a beautiful nymph, Melusine, a creature of the woods and streams. Enchanted that she consented to be his, he swore eternal faith to her, but while she returned his love she also warned him of the terrible penalty if he ever forsook her. She said her foot would suddenly appear to him as a warning, and he would die within three days. Some considerable time later the knight was summoned to Frankfurt to take part in a ceremonial jousting tournament in front of his emperor. Von Staufenberg's prize for his success was the hand in marriage of the emperor's niece, the Duchess of Carinthia. Desperately the knight tried to decline his unwanted bride, but the emperor refused to hear of it. At the marriage celebrations, an exquisite female foot suddenly seemed to penetrate through the wall to the horror of the knight, his bride and their guests. Sadly the knight paid the prophesied penalty by dying shortly afterwards.

The present Schloss Staufenberg is a fortified house, dating back to the seventeenth century, now the vintnery of the Markgräflich Badisches Weingut where you can buy wine or sit at tables in a little outdoor courtyard (indoors in bad weather) to drink and test the new wine and enjoy magnificent views over the vineyards - an experience not to be missed.

The route from Staufenberg continues along the main track, downhill by vines and woods with views to the right across to a particularly handsome traditional farm set in a secluded and sheltered valley. Continue into Durbach, a linear village around road and stream which is an excellent lunch stop for walkers from Oberkirch with a good choice of places to eat. This is the home of the Traminer variety of wine, here called Clevner, and the Klingelberger, better known as Riesling wine.

The Winepath continues directly across from the lane you followed into town. The route goes alongside and turns right behind the town's little white-walled cemetery using a narrow tarmac path. It soon bears left at a white memorial cross and starts climbing. Turn right at a T-junction, the way curving parallel with pylons. Keep on the track as it follows the edge of a wood and continue ahead at the next junction. Look for the signs to Wolfgrube as you walk along the narrow forest track, past a grassy clearance, and then climb steadily through a superb, atmospheric area of forest.

Wolfgrube is one of those typical forest parking, refreshment and, in this case, play areas. The children's playground toys include a little mail-coach in polished wood and there is also an enclosure with deer and a small aviary.

The Winepath now follows a steep and narrow path back into the vines which descend left off the lane to Zell. At a junction turn left towards the wood, following the edge of the wood back towards the vineyards. Turn right at the next junction, by a tall and unusual weathercock, towards Offenburg. This track descends past a viewpoint and sculptures on the left by Hasengrund (**not** as the map shows the route) to join the main road below. Turn left into the centre of Zell Weierbach, to a crossroads by welcoming shops and inns.

The final easy stroll into Offenburg begins by going right at the crossroads but almost immediately forking right into Kühlager, a quiet lane lined by suburban houses and a stream. Where this ends keep in the same direction, still by the stream, along Franz Schmidt Straße almost opposite. As this road bends left to join the main road, take the footpath and cycle way through the fields, straight ahead, which leads into Offenburg. This joins Zeller Strasse, a pleasant road with broad cycle and footway leading to central Offenburg. Keep straight ahead at the traffic island in Schillerplatz, with its attractive statues, to Wilhemstraße alongside the main railway line. Turn left here, going right over the railway bridge and keeping right again in Gütenstraße, to end at the station where an attractive illustrated ceramic wall plaque indicates the official finish (or start) of the Ortenauer Winepath.

Arrange your programme to enjoy at least a short stay in Offenburg and to give yourself enough time to explore this quite charming old wine town which has its own excellent vineyards. You'll find half-timbered and richly decorated baroque houses, street cafés, wine cellars, restaurants and fascinating shops. There is a handsome eighteenth century town hall, a museum in the Ritterhaus, and an impressive baroque church. But particularly delightful on the pedestrianized areas are the street sculptures and fountains. These include the famous Vogelmenschen, half men half bird, who preside good humouredly over Hauptstrasse in the town centre, and a version of the Loch Ness monster whose humps half-buried are visible along the street. Very appropriately, elsewhere in the town there are statues by an Italian sculptor of the two famous gods of wine. Bacchus (in the suburb of Fessenbach) reclines unashamedly at ease, pouring an apparently non-stop stream of wine into his mouth, while Dionysius is surrounded by succulent bunches of grapes which he is also mightily enjoying.

The Clock Carriers' Way

The Clock Carriers' Way is an artificial route in that for the most part it uses official Black Forest Society marked trails to create links between a group of nine Black Forest hotels. These hotels work closely together to transport walkers' luggage and it is an extremely well thought out and well marketed package.

The idea for the route does, however, have roots in historic reality. It goes through the main Black Forest clock making area, and uses many old tracks and ways which undoubtedly would have been walked by seventeenth and eighteenth century clock traders collecting the output of the scores of skilled craftsman from their various workshops in the towns and villages of the southern Black Forest, many of which are visited on this route.

The Clock Carriers' Way also provides perhaps the perfect introduction to the Black Forest, including as it does many spectacularly beautiful and at the same time very typical areas of landscape. It is ideal for anyone who does not wish to take the perhaps more adventurous plunge of attempting one of the major Black Forest Society Hohenwege.

The hotels used are excellent and standards of food and accommodation are extremely high, allowing you to relax in comfort after a long day on forest tracks. Whilst we haven't named all the hotels taking part in the scheme in the text, as they do change from time to time, all are highly recommended.

The route is waymarked with its own special symbol, a red and white clock face on a white background. The frequency of this waymark is spasmodic in places (one problem being that it is avidly collected by the unscrupulous), but in most cases this doesn't really matter because if you are following a Black Forest Society Major Route or Link Path waymarking is likely to be excellent, and you only need look for the appropriate symbol on that particular section.

You can do the route and the hotels in any order or combination, but the classic option is to start from Triberg and go in an anti-clockwise direction to finish either at Triberg (nine days and ten

**CLOCK CARRIERS' WAY
FULL ROUTE**

0 ⸺ 20 km

Schwarzwaldbahn

TRIBERG

KÖNIGSFELD

1. Tag   St Georgen

8. Tag

Schönwald

Brend △

Hasenhof

Gütenbach

Unterkirneck

Furtwangen

7. Tag   VÖHRENBACH

VILLINGEN

Wildgutach

2. Tag   NEUKIRCH

ST MÄRGEN

3. Tag   △ *Hochberg*

Hammereisenbach

Donaueschingen

NEUSTADT   6. Tag   FRIEDENWEILER

Titisee

Titisee   4. Tag

△ *Hochfirst*   Rötenbach

Löffingen

Lenzkirch

Schattenmuhle

Glashütte   5. Tag   Boll

Schluchsee   BONNDORF

73

Waymarks - The Clock Carriers' Way

nights) or at Villingen (seven days and eight nights). But as public transport in the Black Forest is so very good, local trains and inter-linking buses can make it easy quite literally to start or finish at any point you choose.

Bookings can be made direct to the Parkhotel Wehrle, Gartenstr, 24, D-7740 Triberg (Tel: 07722 8602-49); or from the UK via DER Travel Service, 18 Conduit Street, London W1 (Tel: 071 486 4593).

Recommended maps for the whole of the Clock Carriers' Way are HLB/Schwarzwaldverein 1:50,000 Sheet 7 Triberg-Donaueschingen, and Sheet 9 Schluchsee and Wutachtal.

The most detailed guide to the route is *Auf dem Weg der Uhrenträger* written by Rudolf Walz and published by Walz Wanderferien Verlag of Neckartenzlingen. We express our gratitude to Herr Walz for the wealth of detailed information contained in that extremely good and comprehensive book. It is available from Parkhotel Wehrle or local bookshops in the Black Forest. Needless to say any mistakes in our text are entirely our own.

DAY ONE - TRIBERG TO NEUECK
Distance: 21 km   Time: 6¹/₂ hours

Triberg is easily reached by rail on the Black Forest Railway from Offenburg, and this journey perhaps along the Rhine from the North Sea ports via Köln should be a welcome part of anyone's holiday! On the other hand, for a charge of around 132Dm (about £48), Parkhotel Wehrle will arrange transfer for up to four people by taxi from Stuttgart airport if they are notified in advance.

Triberg is a town in a superb, mountainous setting, with a long main street that welcomes the very large numbers of visitors that arrive by coach, car and train. The town often changed hands throughout the centuries, belonging among others to the Lords of Hohenberg who sold it to the Austrian Habsburgs in 1355. It was then managed in turn by up to 30 different noble families before passing to the Margrave of Baden and the Lords of Fürstenberg.

One famous entrepreneurial son of Triberg last century was Johann Evangelist Faller who originally kept an inn, though virtually illiterate. He then took himself off to Russia for some time but returned penniless. Once again he managed to become an innkeeper and traded in spirits, dairy and agricultural products, wood and above all in Black Forest clocks. His inn, Zum Löwen, soon became the unofficial meeting place for all clock traders and clock makers, as well as for traders in many other goods. Faller finally achieved millionaire status with the profits from all these various concerns.

Make sure you find time to visit the excellent Black Forest Museum at the top end of the town, a magnificent collection of artefacts, costumes, models and photographs, beautifully displayed, which bring together many facets of Black Forest life. You'll see a life-sized model of a clock carrier, complete with period costume, broad hat and umbrella, heavy wooden framed pack and an assortment of clocks.

See the museum, if at all possible, the afternoon before you start walking. This is a longish first day, with some climbing, and you'll need to start reasonably early - preferably soon after 9.00am - and aim to be at Martinskapelle or Kolmenhof for lunch if you can. The pilgrimage church of Maria in der Tanne is also worth seeing. The name recalls the original holy picture nailed to a fir tree in the seventeenth century and somehow forgotten until it was unexpectedly rediscovered by Austrian soldiers some 50 years later. One day they heard singing coming from the tree in the wood; the

75

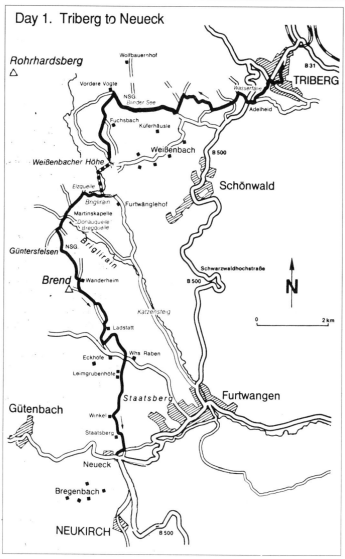

Day 1. Triberg to Neueck

church was built as a result of this and consecrated in 1705. Its style is late baroque and the original holy picture is by the high-altar.

The Clock Carriers' Way starts at the Parkhotel Wehrle, the family-run hotel whose present owner, Herr Klaus Blum, lifelong rambler and hotelier, devised the Clock Carriers' Way. Parkhotel Wehrle is one of the Romantic hotels of the Black Forest. (Romantic is used in the sense of genuine period furnishing and antiques coupled with stylish comfort and modern facilities.) It has a reputation for hospitality and elegant cuisine, with more than 30 ways of serving trout, to give but one example!

Gastronomic delights apart, the real walking begins at the top of the town, at the famous Triberg waterfalls, a series of beautiful white cascades that tumble through a rocky gorge, surrounded by dense woodland where coal-black squirrels leap. Your guest card from the hotel gives free admission to the falls.

There is a rather sad legend connected with the creation of the Triberg waterfalls and a very tall pine tree in the woods. It concerns the beautiful and elegant Countess Gutta who once lost her way some distance from home and was led back to the right path by a handsome, tall young huntsman. Gutta was famous for having a heart of stone and had rejected all offers of marriage. The young huntsman fell desperately in love with her, and finally braved her in her own castle and begged for her hand in marriage. She agreed to be his on one condition and, hardly able to contain his joy, he pleaded to know what this was. On an appointed summer's day he had to leap from the top of the castle rock to a far peak and back again, then he could claim his bride. All the courtiers and servants assembled to witness this amazing attempt and applauded delightedly as the young huntsman successfully took his first leap. Gutta herself began to consider if the return leap was strictly necessary, but before she could restrain him the young man gathered himself for his next attempt and, dazzled by a sudden ray of sunlight, fell to his death into the deep gorge below. His mother, left all alone, cursed the young countess and prophesied that her castle would fall into ruins and she herself would turn to stone. The castle indeed was shortly afterwards totally destroyed and Gutta was turned into a stony series of rocks which became the Triberg waterfalls with their cascades of water rushing furiously down the valley. In memory of Gutta and the huntsman two very tall pines were planted, known as the Guttatanne and the Jägertanne, but lightening destroyed Gutta's tree some years ago.

More prosaically perhaps it was a hydro-electric generator installed at these waterfalls that produced the first street lighting in Germany in 1884. Triberg, incidentally, also had the first ski-lift in the world, installed in 1910.

The waymark for this first part of the walk is the blue diamond with a white flash of a Link Path.

It's a stiff climb to the top of the Triberg waterfalls. At the top car park cross the main road ahead and bear slightly right to pick up the track opposite marked to Schönach. Keep to the right of a little house, Waldesruh, on a narrow path through heather and wood, then after around 100m fork left through more bilberry and heather, curving to a house on the road known as Oberer Adelheid.

Cross directly ahead towards a group of crags and a young fir wood. Continue past some tall firs, keeping ahead under pylons, back into dense forest, still following the blue diamond. The track now follows the edge of the wood, descending slightly to a crossing of tracks about 1 km west of the first pylons. Turn left here, signed to Blindensee, leaving the blue diamonds and dropping down past open fields to another crossroads with trees by a bench - notice the lovely old traditional farm a few metres to the left with its massive roof, Reinertonishofes, which dates from the early seventeenth century.

It might be useful to explain here the purpose behind the extraordinary size of Black Forest farmhouses with their huge, overhanging roofs. During the long, hard winters it was often not easy to leave the farm in order to look after beasts, so everything was contained under that single vast roof, including the store of hay for cattle feed in the great loft space which also acted as insulation. Even the sloping roof was designed to allow snow to slide off easily to the ground, thus creating a wall of heaped-up snow as further insulation.

Turn at the bench and crossroads along a track which soon re-enters the forest. Keep straight ahead along this track which, after about 1 km, descends a shallow valley and curves right. Keep straight ahead at a crossing, taking the ascending track by a bench to join a broader path. Bear left here, again signed for Blindensee, curving round towards a farm. Look out for the entrance to a nature reserve, marked by a large black eagle sign 'Naturschutzgebiet.' This leads

Donauquelle - source of the Danube

along a boardwalk through the reserve, past an intriguing landscape of tall heathers and dwarf pines and peat bog, and around the Blindensee itself which is a small, deep, still peaty lake.

There is an old story that says that every year on St Bartholomew's day a rivulet escapes from the Blindensee threatening to drown the valley, but the Virgin prevents this from happening with a miraculous net. In prosaic reality the water level remains at a constant 10m irrespective of weather conditions.

The boardwalk ends in a narrow path which leads to a tarmac farm road. Turn left here. This is now the Westweg, Europe's oldest long distance path, and for the rest of the day the red diamond waymark marks the route. The lane passes open fields and when it turns into a farm, Varderer Voigte, left, the Way swings right along a track by pasture and forest. As this track bears left towards a farm, the Westway bears left by pylons, well marked. It goes into forest, swinging left again along a lovely stretch of heathery path beside the edge of the wood, then going more deeply into the wood and finally emerging at a track which leads to the road. Ahead is a crossroads and small shelter at Weissenbacher Höher.

The Westweg takes a narrow path to the right which follows the edge of the wood, by Vogte Farm. Go right at the farm track, then first left uphill along the valley. After just under a kilometre, and well before the track meets the road, look for another narrow track which forks in from the left - this is easy to miss as the waymarks are ambiguous. The Westweg climbs back up this track past Elzquelle, a spring and source of the River Elz, a tributary of the Rhine. Keep following the track until it joins a lane which you take to the crossroads by the Martinskapelle Inn with the St Martin's Chapel itself (a forest chapel dating from the thirteenth century) a couple of hundred metres ahead.

The farmhouse nearby has altered little since the eighteenth century and has a traditional old kitchen which visitors are sometimes shown. Close by, and just below the Kilmenhof Inn, is a spring which is the source of the River Danube (celebrated as the immortal 'Blue Danube' by Johann Strauss); an unremarkable spot for the birth of one of Europe's mighty rivers, a river which crosses Germany, Austria and Hungary to reach Russia and the Black Sea. Steps lead down to the little spring itself.

The Westweg continues from the crossroads reached before the chapel - a path leads off marked to Brend. This is a beautiful section, a steady climb along a path which suddenly becomes quite rocky, a way over large stones and between trees, occasionally tricky to see as you wind between boulders. Just keep in the same direction, over the first summit and on to join a broader track past the Naturfreunde hostel.

The summit of Brend (1,149m above sea level) lies to the right and is a

Vogelmensch, Offenburg (Day 3 Ortenauer Winepath).

Rankmühle - traditional farm with barn roof.

magnificent viewpoint over the rolling Black Forest hills, particularly from the stone viewing tower. If it is clear you can see across to such peaks as Belchen, Kandel, Feldberg, Hochfirst and the Simonwälder Forest. There is an inn by the tower with local specialities on offer.

The path from Brend goes through the wood, a few metres back from but parallel to the tarmac road. It rejoins the road after about a kilometre. Follow the lane by open pasture as it descends to a bend by a wood where, a short distance from the Goldener Rabe Inn, the Westweg turns left along a farm track towards Leimgrabenhof Farm. The Way takes a track into the forest - keep straight ahead into the forest to the farm at Winkel from where it bears left along a grassy track which curves towards Staatberg Farm, the track continuing along a low ridge with fine views down to Furtwangen. At a crossing path follow the Westweg right for Neueck with its hotels. Paths also link Furtwangen and Neukirch from this point.

DAY TWO - NEUECK TO ST MARGEN
Distance: 12 km   Time: 4 hours

This is a very much shorter and easier day than the first. We recommend that you combine it with a visit to the superb German National Clock Museum at Furtwangen, easily reached by bus from Neueck or Neukirch. The bus leaves for Furtwangen via Neukirch soon after 9.00am, returning to Neueck around or soon after 11.00am (remember to wait on the other side of the road). This gives ample time to enjoy this unique museum which will explain so much about the skill and ingenuity of the Black Forest clock makers and their traditions which still live on in precision engineering. There will still be ample time to complete this easy but spectacular walk.

From Neueck a farm road runs from the junction by the bus-stop signed to Fallengrund. This stretch of the Clock Carriers' Way is marked with a red diamond on a yellow ground, being part of the Kaisterstuhl-Rhein Traverse Route. This is easy, gentle walking past meadow and forest. Keep ahead on the lane as it emerges from the wood and curves down towards Fallengrund. You fork before the

Waterfall in Rötenbachschlucht

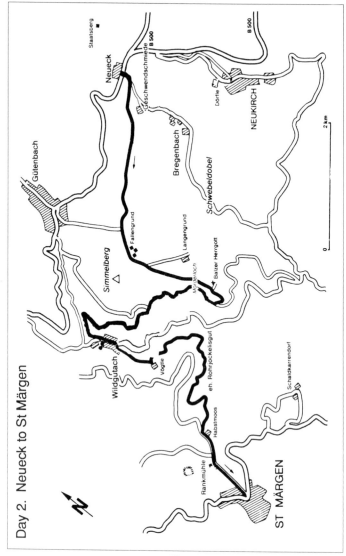

Day 2. Neueck to St Märgen

The Balzer Herrgott - portrait of Christ in a living tree

farm up a stony track, and at the next crossroads and route-board the
Clock Carriers' Way heads left towards Balzer Herrgott.

*Balzer Herrgott, when you reach it, is a wayside shrine, an ancient beech
tree within which a face of Christ has been absorbed into the trunk of the
living tree. Originally, about a hundred years ago, there was in fact a
wrought iron cross with the figure of Christ; but as the trunk grew round it
the solution seemed to be to remove the cross piece and now only the head and
shoulders of the Christ are visible. Annually more of the figure disappears
and the sandstone carvings crumble a little more.*

Keep in the same direction, following the forest path left, but soon
fork left down a steep and stony path (quite dramatic) which descends
through the forest into Wild Gutach, a deep ravine. You emerge at a
track, Gütenstraße. Turn right, following the track which goes above
the deep, densely wooded valley for about a kilometre before turning
left (waymarked) along a track which elbows back down the valley
and descends to the isolated village in the valley bottom. Cross the
river by the wood yard to the comfortable little Löwen Inn, the only
available lunch and refreshment stop which is closed on Thursdays,

so that if you are here on that day make sure you bring plenty of supplies with you.

The route from Wild Gutach is easy enough to find. Follow the narrow lane by the church, Kirchstraße, which climbs steadily up the side of the valley. There are fine views as you climb and the occasional bench to enjoy them from. The lane curves around the valley and then becomes a stony track climbing steadily upwards, going on the shoulder of the gorge through dense woodland. Keep in the same direction, eventually passing a little shelter and spring and curve round a great headland above the valley before finally emerging on a farm track. Keep ahead at a crossroads past the Rankmühle, a picturesque old water-mill and farmhouse used in the *Black Forest Clinic* television series. Walk directly ahead along the narrow farm road which crosses pasture to lead into the village of St Märgen.

St Märgen is a small, compact upland resort with a truly magnificent little twin-towered baroque church. The church has an unusual statue of the Virgin Mary which is actually medieval in origin but wears some very striking, rich baroque robes. The eye is inevitably drawn to this statue, surrounded by the rays of a gilt halo and standing in the side chapel where it is positioned at the apex of the altar.

St Märgen also has a special breed of horse, brown with white manes and known as St Märgen Füchse, which were used to drag the huge pine and fir tree trunks out of the forest. The horses were superseded by tractors and other heavy equipment, but are now enjoying something of a revival as people realise that they do far less harm to the environment.

DAY THREE - ST MÄRGEN TO NEUSTADT
Distance: 25 km   Time: 7 hours

This is another longish day but with some attractive walking; an early start is essential!

Leave St Märgen on the Neustadt road, eastwards, but soon branch left along a tree-lined track which dips across a beck. Once again you are following the blue diamond with a white flash of a Link Path. At a children's playground veer left along the path signed to Neuhäusel, then bear right into the forest. Keep right with the blue waymarks at

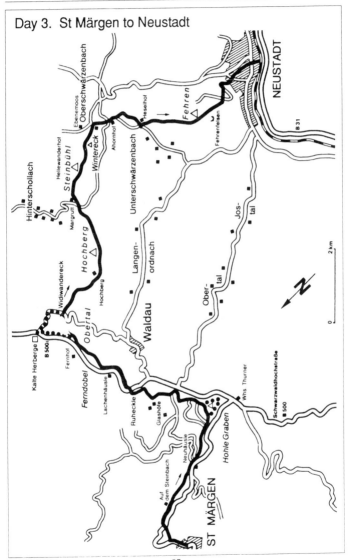

Day 3. St Märgen to Neustadt

the next fork. This approaches the main road from St Märgen, but then swings back into the wood. Keep with the signs to Neuhäusel and Thurner. At a T-junction turn left, parallel to the road, emerging at the roadside by a delightful notice-board that tells of a wild pig discovering litter left by visitors in the wood and asking his wife to come and share his joy at finding he must have relatives living in a nearby town!

Cross the road, continuing on the other side along a path parallel to the road which emerges at a bus-stop and inn, Auf dem Steinbach, by a road junction. The Way continues by a small building from this junction, in the same direction but along a green track parallel to the road. This is clearly a pre-Motor Age road, almost certainly one used by clock carriers, which climbs by forest and over a low ridge (fine views) before rejoining the road at Hornberg. The Way continues again on the left of the present road, at first a grassy path that climbs the ridge once more, then passes through a small wood and open fields before rejoining the road yet again. Follow the road for a short distance to the next junction where you take a track left between a branching lane and the road signed to Gasthof Kreuz. The track climbs through the wood past fields to emerge at the inn, with its maypole and fascinating inn sign.

You are now back on the Westweg with the red diamond on white waymark. Exit from the inn yard, follow the track left by an impressive old farm but turn right across the field to a lane where the Way bears right, back towards the main road. As you near the road, turn left along Kohlplatz and follow the narrow farm road left. Pass the first gate, but just before the second turn sharp right across on a field path at right-angles, well signed, heading towards a wood through which the path curves left to the lane. Turn right, walk along the lane for about 500m to the next junction where you turn left along Ruheckle for another 400m to reach the main road. Cross the road and almost directly opposite is a narrow path through the wood to a little inn, Lachenhäusle, an excellent morning coffee stop - but closed on Mondays.

The path goes alongside the right-hand side of the road (NOT the forest track that plunges downhill right) for 200m before dipping into the wood. Where the track swings right, look out for a narrow path

View from the Mittelweg

through deep undergrowth straight ahead - this is in fact the Westweg. Keep ahead now, still parallel with the road, to emerge at a parking place by a TV relay station. The Clock Carriers' Way actually cuts off the corner along the track which bears right at this point, but it is worth continuing on the Westweg for another kilometre as it passes through an attractive section of woodland and then heads alongside the wood before swinging down to the road near Kalte Herberge.

The little inn at Kalte Herberge is at the watershed of Europe - rain that falls on the western side of its roof runs down to join the Rhine and end in the North Sea, that which falls on the eastern side goes into the Danube and ends up in the Black Sea.

Retrace your steps, but this time bear left along the narrow lane which carries another famous Black Forest Hohenweg - the Mittelweg - a white flash on a red diamond being its waymark. The lane climbs up the side of a narrow valley, first woodland and then pasture, before joining the main Clock Carriers' Way and turning left along a broad forest track signed to the Engel Inn. Easy, level walking now along a broad track for 2 km to the Engel (Angel), a delightful,

Vordermargrutt - traditional farm with barn roof

traditional Black Forest country inn, little changed over the centuries and with simple but excellent food on offer.

Continue along the track in the same direction over the gentle summit of the Hochberg (1,116m), emerging in an open area of woodland notable in late summer for the elderberry bushes with their vivid scarlet berries.

Ahead is a large clearing containing a magnificent farmhouse with a truly massive roof barn - the Vordermargrutt. The Mittelweg passes behind the farm and continues along a stony track into the wood, forking left with the waymarks and climbing steadily over Steinbühl summit. As you descend there are glimpses of a quite delightful traditional farmhouse, Hellenmanderhof, in its sheltered pasture, contained within the forest. Keep ahead, the path meandering on the edge of the wood before bearing to the right and emerging out of the wood at Schwärzenbach, by a cross-country skiing base and a parking place, close by a cross commemorating the Russian soldiers who died in the Napoleonic wars.

Nearby is also an atonement cross which dates from the fifteenth or sixteenth century. It was a medieval tradition that when one person accidentally killed another in a fight, the sinner had to wear a penitent's garment and, with bare breast or sometimes even naked, had to walk to the victim's grave with a candle that had been deliberately extinguished. Once there he had to call on the dead person by name, then lie on the grave till permitted to arise by the victim's relatives. Sometimes even his own relatives had to kneel in church until they too were allowed to rise in their turn. The accused also had to pay a fine either in money or goods and defray such expenses as a doctor's bill.

The Mittelweg crosses to the narrow lane ahead but, immediately past a tall wayside cross, bears right down a narrow path which leads through a small wood to join a lane by another old farm and more shrines. Keep left to the junction with the main road. Cross here, the Way now following a broad track used for cross-country skiing. There is so much skiing in this section of forest and so many routes and waymarks for walkers and skiers, that you must look carefully for the red diamond with the white flash waymark at every junction. At the first fork keep left through glades of tall firs. Keep ahead at the next crossing of tracks, your track eventually joining a broader one from Kleineisenbach by some shooting huts. These are soon left behind as the Way bears right back into the forest, climbing steadily past another crossroads to a T-junction. Turn right here with the Neustadt signs, the track climbing over another low summit to emerge at a grillplatz and fine viewpoint at the end of the ridge on the Tannenberg. The track now curves sharply downhill to a road junction above the youth hostel. Turn sharp right down a narrow tarmac way which cuts by the road-ends and along Amselweg. Keep ahead to the centre of Neustadt, emerging at the bottom of the town below the church.

Neustadt is another extremely attractive town with a fascinating history because of its importance in coaching days; a link that survives with the Adler Post Hotel which has been kept by the same family since mail-coach times. Crowded into a narrow valley and built on different levels to maximise the use of space, it has an impressive church, some interesting old buildings and shops, a museum, narrow streets and passageways, and it is, not surprisingly, a popular and busy tourist centre.

DAY FOUR - NEUSTADT TO BONNDORF
Distance: 22 km   Time: 6 hours

From the Adler Post Hotel in Neustadt make your way down to the bottom of the town and keep ahead past a delightful statue of a Narrenfigur (jester) to the railway station. Past the station, cross the tracks at the level-crossing and keep ahead under the high concrete bridge carrying the B31 road. Bear left at a fork along Färbeweg. After around 130m take the path left, by a wooden notice, which follows a stream parallel to the road and passes a spring and little waterfall on the left. The path, narrow, climbs steeply through dense forest, but with strategically placed benches for a breather. Where you meet a broad track, cross to pick up the path directly ahead, ascending steeply but steadily through the wood until you are almost at a car park at Saiger Kreuz where the path to Hochfirst summit bears off left. Go across the lane, continuing along the path which bends left through dense wood to reach the summit at 1,000m above sea level.

Because of the trees there is not much view from here, unless you ascend the tall metal tower which combines as a viewpoint and TV station. A circular staircase takes you to the top balcony from where in fine weather there are superb views across Lake Titisee, the Feldberg and the hills beyond. The staircase is narrow, dark and can be somewhat claustrophobic and there is a small charge for the climb, payable to the Black Forest Society. Near the tower is an inn and you will probably feel you have deserved an early break after the ascent.

From Hochfirst the Clock Carriers' Way now follows the Mittelweg again - the red diamond with a white flash. This is a beautiful forest path, Black Forest rambling at its finest along a thickly wooded ridge with glimpses of sky and the occasional glint of water. Wayfinding is easy for the next 2.5 km. Just after the point where the Mittelweg turns sharp right, look for the fork in the paths where you leave the Mittelweg to the left and take another of the Big Four routes, the Freiburg-Bodensee Traverse, marked by an attractive red and white diamond on a yellow ground.

This again is easy, attractive walking, this time on a broader forest track. After about 2 km look for the point where the route cuts off a corner of the main forest track, descending to the right before

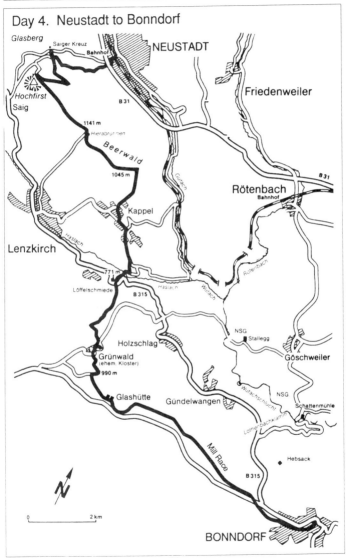

Day 4. Neustadt to Bonndorf

Along the Mühlenbachweg near Bonndorf

emerging into open pasture above the valley and the village of Kappel. Where the tarmac lane, as the track has now become, turns sharp left with the edge of the forest, the path is directly ahead over the fields down to Kappel. Follow the lane into the village, turning left at the main crossroads and heading through the village (refreshments available), past the little church with its onion dome.

Keep ahead until you join the main road. As the road bends left at Gasthaus Stern, the way is ahead along a quiet lane. After about 400m turn left down Grünwaldstraße - note an interesting garden with fossil ammonites on the right. Another 600m now, but look for a small white marble wayside cross, opposite which a grassy track marked 'Zu Mühlweg' descends into the valley. Take this, keeping left at a fork along Mühlweg, and straight ahead at a crossing. The path, now a stony track, descends into a little wooded ravine. At the road at the bottom cross the bridge over the little Haslach river, but immediately go sharp right along a path signed to Löffelschmied which climbs up the other slide, under the arches of the bridge carrying the long closed Bonndorf railway.

Ahead is the inn, Löffelschmied, whose name means literally The Spoon Smithy, indicating the site of an old forge where spoons were manufactured centuries ago. Spoon manufacturing was another popular cottage industry in the Black Forest. The inn is a highly recommended lunch stop, serving the excellent local Lenzkirch beer, but it is closed on Wednesdays.

The Clock Carriers' Way continues by following the main road for a few metres then turning right up the stony forest track at the far side of the bridge over the stream. This ascends along the side of a wooded gorge, eventually zig-zagging round to emerge at Grünwald, a hamlet in a forest clearing which once had a monastery but now has two inns (in case you didn't stop at Löffelschmied) and a little church.

The Way, now sharing the blue diamond of a Link Path, continues along the lane past the church, but where the lane bends sharply right it continues ahead onto a forest track which climbs steadily through the edge of the forest. After a kilometre look for the branching path left marked to Glashütte, the name a link with the old Black Forest glass industry, where there's a bus shelter and an inn.

The path to Bonndorf, again marked with the blue diamond, follows the lane in front of the inn and then bears off left through young forest. Keep ahead at all crossings; easy level walking, well waymarked with the blue diamond. After about 3 km the path (marked) veers left, away from the broader forest track you are now following. After another 500m you pass a spring on the left, the Scharmätzelbrunnen, which is the start of an old mill race where the path (marked) veers off the forest track to follow the little canalised stream - a beautiful, atmospheric path of pine needles, green moss, ferns and trees.

Another 3 km of easy walking brings you to a parking area by a busy road junction on the outskirts of Bonndorf. Cross the road and take the quieter road into town to your right (Bierbrunnen) under pylons, soon turning left along Waldstraße which leads into the town centre for your hotel.

Bonndorf is a clean, quiet little town and resort on the edge of the Black Forest with a long, winding main street and a little park.

DAY FIVE - BONNDORF TO FRIEDENWEILER
Distance: 18 km   Time: 5 hours

This is perhaps the most spectacular day on the Clock Carriers' Way because it includes part of the Gutachschlucht (the Gutach gorge), one of the most impressive natural features in the whole of the Black Forest. You are unlikely to pass refreshment places in the middle of the day, so it is sensible to carry a packed lunch or at least emergency supplies for this section.

From the centre of Bonndorf follow the main street, Martinstraße, as it bends through the town curving right at a junction past a supermarket before which a lane, Bergstraße, branches off left (there is also a sign to the Philosophenweg). Bergstraße climbs fairly steeply. At the traffic restriction sign keep ahead with the blue diamond with white flash Link Path signs, this time heading for Hebsack and Lothenbachklamm.

You are soon crossing open fields with extensive views across farm and forest, a pleasant change from the enclosed forest tracks of yesterday. The Way curves left to a wayside cross; at the fork keep left with the blue diamond, under pylons, but as the farm track bends sharp left continue straight ahead on a path across the fields. Head for the grey pylon and the farm at Hebsack ahead, picking up a clear line of path which goes to the left-hand side of the farm where you turn sharp right before the farmhouse and go round the outside. Keep in the same direction to pick up a field track which dwindles to a path heading for a small wood. After going around the wood the path descends to the crossroads at a parking place on the B315 Bonndorf-Lenzkirch road. Turn right into the main road, cross the bridge towards Lenzkirch over the stream but go sharp right at the end of the bridge.

This path is a narrow rocky way which drops suddenly and sharply into the Lothenbachklamm (the Lothenbach gorge), a narrow and rocky ravine down which the path twists with footbridges and handrails - great care is needed - alongside a spectacular series of cataracts.

You eventually emerge at a car park by the Schattenmühle bridge in the centre of Wutachtal. The Schattenmühle (Mill in the Shadows), a traditional farmhouse, is at the far side of the bridge on the right.

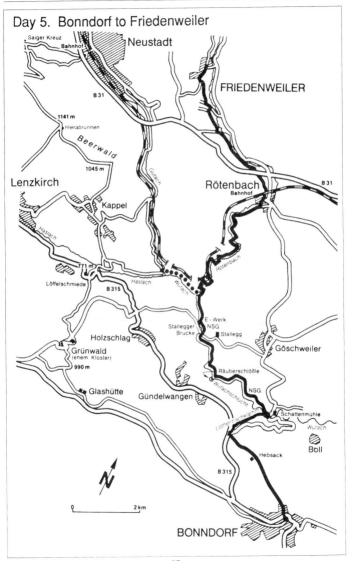

Day 5. Bonndorf to Friedenweiler

The inn alongside it is an excellent morning coffee stop, the only refreshment place until Rötenbach. The Clock Carriers' Way continues from the footpath by the bridge, now with the red and white diamond on yellow background waymark of the Freiburg-Bodensee Traverse Route. The path ascends by steps, finally reaching a forest track on the rim of the gorge and giving intriguing views into the wooded depths below.

The Wutach - its name meaning 'fierce and angry,' a testimony to the force of its rushing water - is now a nature reserve of national importance for its wildlife - wildflowers, birds, mammals and butterflies. It was, however, almost lost some years ago under a major reservoir flooding scheme which was successfully opposed by the Black Forest Society.

Follow the track for about 2 km, passing an interesting spring on the right filled with tufa - rock-like limestone deposited by the stream which drains from the limestone-rich countryside in the plateau above the gorge. At a fork bear left, across a shallow dip, keeping ahead on a path through the woods which crosses a low headland to a stream where the Way bears left again, zig-zagging up to join a broader path coming in from the right. This curves round back into the main valley, becoming a narrow way on the rim of the gorge. A path from the valley bottom joins it. Look for a rock path with a handrail, left, which leads to the Räuberschlößle, (The Robbers' Castle), a crag towering high above the valley floor which is both a superb viewpoint and natural resting place.

Retrace your steps to the main path and continue along the Traverse Route up the valley for another 2 km, the path gradually losing height to descend closer to the valley. You reach an enclosed bridge across the Wutach, the Stallegg Brücke. Do not cross, keep on the same side on the track which curves to the right alongside the river, passing the remarkable 49m-high Stallegg Tanne fir tree, one of the tallest trees in the valley. Continue past a small hydro-electric power station with a viewing platform. The Stalleger Kraftwerk was built by the Lords of Fürstenberg and provided Donaueschingen with electricity until fairly recently. It is now an industrial monument. The path finally descends to the riverside and a delightful picnic area near the confluence of the two rivers that make up the Wutach - the Haslach and the Rötenbach.

The Clock Carriers' Way now follows the Rötenbach gorge, turning right immediately over the Rötenbach and following a narrow path over a series of footbridges, some of them a shade rickety, to ascend this little valley, past waterfalls.

This is an extraordinarily beautiful stretch of walking in a narrow secluded river valley through which the footpath runs on alternate banks. It's an area rich in wildflowers and birdlife, and the occasional sudden rumble nearby is caused by the trains on the twisting Schwarzwaldbahn (Black Forest Railway) which runs immediately behind and above the valley to your left.

Wayfinding is easy enough through this gorge. Follow the blue diamonds of a Link Path for about 3m, keeping ahead at a broad crossing track, the railway eventually becomes close enough to see passing trains. At last the path swings right over a bridge onto a track near a small red sandstone quarry. This track leads directly ahead into Rötenbach, a compact village with a little square town hall, well supplied with comfortable inns and eating houses.

For the route to Friedenweiler, a section only marked with the Clock Carriers' waymark, (but well marked), this begins by following Friedenweiler Straße to the left towards the station, then bears left along Ganterstraße, the waymark on lampposts. Keep directly ahead along a farm track which takes the underpass under the main B31 road. At a fork keep slightly right by a fence along the Ackerweg signed to Josefhütte, a shelter soon passed. Keep ahead towards the woodland - at the next fork bear right. At a T-junction turn right towards another little shooting hut, a lovely grass way between trees. A kilometre ahead is another junction where you keep right again, always keeping in this north-westerly direction up the Klosterbach Valley.

A small pool in which to refresh the feet lies at the end of the wood, and a farm track curves towards the village of Friedenweiler straight ahead. You pass a barn and farm at Maierhof before reaching the lane which swings into Friedenweiler, with a magnificent view across to its monastery set against a backcloth of trees, near the village centre.

This area is associated with Martin Blessing, the celebrated Orchestrion maker who learnt much of his craft in Russia and sold his greatest masterpiece in London for the then astounding sum of 15,000 gulden. So famous was his expertise that living composers wrote specially for his instrument, and as the last of the Blessing dynasty was buried Mozart's "Misere" was played on an Orchestrion.

DAY SIX - FRIEDENWEILER TO VOHRENBACH
Distance: 18 km   Time: 5 hours

After the drama and splendours of the Wutach this day's walk may come as something of an anticlimax.. This is pleasant rather than memorable rambling, but with a few real highlights. A fairly easy day to take a little time over, after previous exertions.

From Friedenweiler village follow Klosterstraße then Schwimmbadstraße north-westwards out of the village centre past the little forest Lido - swimming pool and boating lake - to the main road. After 100m along the road take the track into the forest, right, known as Kirchweg, once again following the familiar blue diamond Link Path waymark. You soon reach a three-way fork - Kirchweg is the middle of the three, a long forest track steadily climbing. Its name, Church Way, indicates the fact that in former times people from Eisenbach, the next village, used the path each Sunday to go to church at Friedenweiler.

The track ascends eventually passing a cross, Brandkreuz, in a clearing. This was erected to commemorate a terrible forest fire which took place in 1784 and required the efforts of 3,000 people to control it. Keep directly ahead past the shooting hut back into the forest. After a further 2 km, having kept directly ahead at several crossings, the route emerges in the Black Forest equivalent of a New Town - Auf der Höchst, a settlement of modern factories and new suburban houses. At the main crossroads turn left (new development has changed the paths here) along the road past factories for 300m, then turn right into a suburban road which curves round to the left to another crossroads. Turn right here along a track named Glaserweg and a keep fit route. Keep ahead into the wood, soon picking up the blue diamond waymarks again. Follow signs for Bubenbach. This path becomes another very attractive forest track, gradually curving to the right above Eisenbach before descending gently into Bubenbach

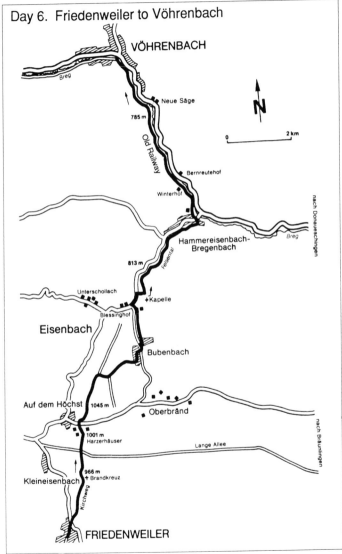

Day 6. Friedenweiler to Vöhrenbach

VÖHRENBACH

Breg

Neue Säge

785 m

Old Railway

Bernreutehof

Winterhof

Hammereisenbach-
Bregenbach

Breg

nach Donaueschingen

813 m

Reiserntal

Unterschollach

+ Kapelle

Blessinghof

Eisenbach

Bubenbach

Auf dem Höchst   1045 m

Oberbränd

1001 m
Harzerhäuser

Lange Allee

nach Bräunlingen

966 m
+ Brandkreuz

Kleineisenbach

Kirchweg

FRIEDENWEILER

N

0   2 km

where it becomes a tarmac lane into a charming village with traditional houses, their balconies dripping with flowers. Pass a crucifix on the left on Thomasweg, fork half-right into Bubenbachstrasse and left to the church.

From here turn right along Kohlwaldstraße (obviously another charcoal burning area in former times), then bear left into Schulweg past the village school. This lane thins to a track up the valley, parallel with the road along the edge of a wood. Follow this for a kilometre to Blessinghof, a crossroads where the Bär Inn provides an excellent coffee stop (closed Tuesdays).

Continue along the main road for 250m (you can avoid walking along the busy road by cutting through the saw works on the left) before crossing to a track on the right-hand side which runs parallel to the road. This is in fact a delightful way through broom, heather and, in early summer, lupins. The main road is rejoined again at Felsental where it has to be followed for the last kilometre into Hammereisenbach. The name of this somewhat elongated village recalls the existence in former times of a hammer making factory in the forest, belonging to the Counts of Fürstenberg.

The Urachtal Valley, which comes in from the left, was also the home of several famous local clock makers. The Hammer Inn is also an excellent place for lunch, renowned for its excellent trout at remarkably reasonable prices (closed Mondays).

From the Hammer Inn turn right into Fürstenbergweg across the playing field and past a cottage by the forest edge. Keep on the lower path by pylons and a chain-link fence. At the crossroads go left across the wooden bridge over the Eisenbach stream and cross the main road.

The final part of the walk into Vöhrenbach follows the old Donaueschingen-Furtwangen railway line. This is reached by the track to the left by the Felsen Gasthaus with its rabbit farm behind the inn, following the banks of the River Breg. This is easy, level walking as you would expect along an old railway track, with just a few odd buildings and platelayers' huts to remind you of its purpose. You cross the Lindach stream close by the Kohlbrücke bridge, the Clock Carriers' Way now shared with the Bregtalweg, a local waymarked route through the Breg Valley. River, main road and former railway share the narrow valley, enclosed within steep, thickly wooded slopes.

This is pleasant rather than dramatic walking, passing the crossroads with the Fohnrenschachen Valley on the right, curving with the main valley into Vöhrenbach. About 5 km from Kohlbrücke you will reach Vöhrenbach's old station, now a small industrial site. Keep to your left, picking out the line of the old railway on the left as it continues past the station. The path becomes now much narrower and more like a railway track; a Link Path swings right into the town centre and bus station in the square.

Vöhrenbach is a town whose history goes back to the thirteenth century. It has strong links, particularly from the nineteenth century, with clock making and the construction of mechanical organs. There are a number of fine half-timbered buildings, including the Gasthaus Kreuz which, although recently restored, dates from the seventeenth century.

DAY SEVEN - VÖHRENBACH TO VILLINGEN
Distance: 17 km Time: 5 hours

From Vöhrenbach church cross the main road into Kälbergäßle opposite the Gasthaus Kreuz - once again following the blue diamond with white flash Link Path waymark. Keep ahead along a tarmac lane by open pasture which climbs above the Langenbach Valley, passing a series of small factories which show how manufacturing industry still flourishes in the Black Forest.

After a kilometre the lane curves into Langenbach village below. Bear right past a factory entrance to the Gasthof Hirschen at a crossroads. The Clock Carriers' Way now keeps straight ahead (ignore the road left) up a stony track past fields, signed to St Georgen. The path climbs to a bench at a cross and soon swings steeply uphill towards the forest ahead.

Once in the forest the gradient eases slightly, but it is still a steady pull up the ridge known as Schöneck along a typical forest track. The path levels and the forest thins to young woodland and scrub - keep ahead along a narrower grassy way back into the wood, then back into scrub and young firs. The path finally opens out into lovely high

Day 7. Vöhrenbach to Villigen

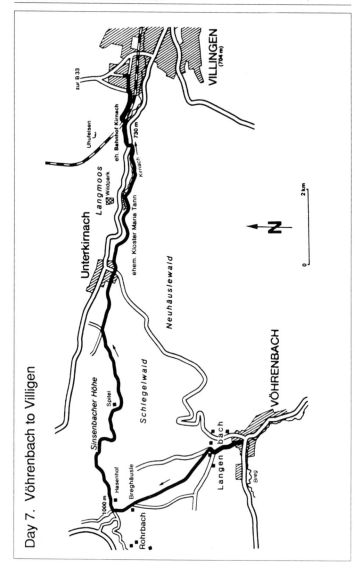

pasture. On the left is Breghäusle, farm and inn (closed Mondays). As you join the lane at the crossroads the inn is to your left, should you decide on a coffee stop. Otherwise keep ahead for another 500m to the next rather complex crossroads. The Clock Carriers' Way turns right along what is in fact the second forest road on the right, marked to Am Schlegelberg.

Follow this track along the ridge, opening out to a clearance with extensive views towards the Schlegelwald below, to a crossroads with a crucifix fixed on a high wooden pole. Fork half-left here along the forest track marked with both Link Path and Clock Carriers' waymarks, soon heading back into the trees. The track contours above the Reichenbach Valley; bear half-right at a fork curving round past some handsome tall pines and descending gradually above the Sinbach Valley, the Way now bearing to the right.

The Way now comes close to the edge of the wood, looking across the pastures of the Uhlbach with views of a fine traditional farm with its duck pond and pastures enclosed by the trees. Keep the same direction, local waymarks with a W or F2 marking the way. The path bears slightly right as you re-enter the heart of the forest then, after another 600m follows the edge of the forest again in a sharp left then right bend before finally emerging onto a tarmac track at a little waterworks on the low ridge above Roggenbach. Follow this lane down, along the ridge, into Unterkirnach, descending past the cemetery, wild plant botanic park and school to the Unterkirnach church. Follow the waymarked path immediately left in front and past the fountain to the village centre and the Rössl Inn.

Unterkirnach was, in the last century, a centre for manufacture of Orchestrions, those remarkable mechanical musical machines that pre-dated the gramophone.

From the Rössl Inn cross the road and go along Rossackerweg which leads to the underpass under the new main road flyover. Go under here, turning left (still along Rossackerweg) and following the red ladybird waymark. This is a deviation off the Clock Carriers' Way but well worth taking. At the end of the tarmac is a delightful little dual arm fountain on the right.

Take the left fork at the fountain into the forest, keeping with the ladybird signs along a high-level track above the Kirnach Valley. This soon opens out to give views across the valley. Bear left at a fork with the ladybird, then keep ahead until the track hairpins around a crossing stream over a bridge. Immediately past this take the sharp left fork back alongside the stream, now with a fir tree waymark. This gradually loses height to rejoin the track along the valley floor, just past the former Kirnachtal monastery and close to a tiny graveyard with simple linked crosses over the graves.

Keep ahead on this track now. Where it appears to go directly over a bridge ahead, your way is to keep right alongside the riverbank on an attractive path which also carries the Schwarzwald-Jura-Bodensee Way, the waymark a green diamond on a yellow ground. This is now the waymark to be followed until Villingen. The path broadens and emerges at an extraordinary tree-fountain, the Romäus spring, reputed to be water of such pure quality that Villingen people to this day collect it in cans and containers to make the most excellent tea.

Romäus was reputed to be a friendly local giant, much liked by the people of Villingen, who after a time became somewhat conceited and fell foul of the authorities. They tricked him into captivity and he was flung into a deep dungeon from where he eventually managed to escape. The people of Villingen took him to their hearts again and he lived a long and happy life (in some versions of the tale he distinguishes himself in battle where he meets his end).

Look for the waymarks on the left of the path running parallel to the lane through the wood. You will emerge just before the junction with the main road. Cross and turn left into the main road for a few metres, walk over the bridge to locate the path at the far side of the Kirnach river. In spite of the roar of traffic on the main road, this is a delightful path through a lovely area of woodland, by a stream and waterfalls. It emerges at a memorial to Hubert Gantler, Head Forester in the area from 1876-1895 and a pioneer conservationist who also laid out many of the paths through the forest.

The path reaches Kirnach-Villingen station which is now closed to passenger traffic. A path alongside the railway line leads directly, between railway and river, into the Villingen town centre.

If you are staying at Kurcafé Bosse in Germanswald, cross the railway at the level-crossing at the far side of the station. Almost opposite a red heart by some steps marks the path which runs along the edge of Germanswald wood, parallel to the road. Follow this, keeping to the path beyond the crossroads at the edge of the forest until you reach the junction and bus-stop where Oberer Waldstraße bears off right. Oberförster Ganter Straße on which Kurcafé Bosse lies is around 400m down this road on the left.

One advantage of ending your walk on the Clock Carriers' Way at Villingen is that you can explore this superb old town before catching a train over the Höllental line (via Donaueschingen and Neustadt) to Freiburg for inter-city trains to Köln and the Dutch ports.

In any event give yourself several hours to discover Villingen, easily reached by bus or taxi from Kurcafé Bosse. This is a perfectly preserved old walled town, with turreted town gates, a beautiful minster, an old town hall, a town museum (with many antique clock makers' workshops and several Black Forest clocks), a Franciscan museum and streets of old houses, shops and inns. Close by the minster is a remarkable bronze sculpture showing the long history of the town; the figures and plaques relating key events are executed with passion and considerable humour.

Back to Triberg

Whilst for the purpose of this book the lovely old town of Villingen did seem to make a logical end to the Clock Carriers' Way, the route does allow a return to Triberg by an additional two days of walking, staying overnight at Königsfeld. This also forms an optional part of the Clock Carriers' Way package.

If you do decide to do this, which is highly recommended, Day Eight is from Villingen to Königsfeld, a total of 16 km requiring an estimated time of four hours. Königsfeld has an interesting history as it was given to a Protestant group called the Brothers of Unity by the Württemberg dynasty with certain privileges attached. The church has separate seating for men and women, and the seats are arranged lengthways so that the preacher can be clearly seen by everybody. In the graveyard the graves belonging to the Brothers display no titles or words of remembrance, solely an individual's place of origin, name, date of birth and death. Albert Schweitzer, the great mathematician, physicist and musician, was born here and played the organ in the church.

The route is easy enough to find from Villingen back to Kirnach station and then on the Link Path through the Brigach Valley to rejoin the Jura-Bodensee Traverse Route as far as Stockwald. From here the Clock Carriers' Way takes a cross-country route via the Gasthaus Grossbauer Linde, Schoren and the Rotwald forest.

An alternative, shorter route (giving more time to see Villingen) would be to follow the well marked Ostweg direct from Villingen via Mönchweiler.

The route on Day Nine from Königsfeld back to Triberg (20 km, estimated journey time 5¹/₂ hours) uses the Link Path (blue diamond white flash), from Königsfeld via Bregnitz and Kleinmoosh to join the Lahr-Rotweil Traverse (red and blue diamond on a yellow background) before branching off at Bopper on the Link Path (blue diamond white flash) that descends to Triberg and Parkhotel Wehrle.

There is a detailed description of this part of the route in *Auf dem Weg der Uhrenträger* by Rudolf Walz, whilst a brief English language synopsis of the route is available from any of the hotels taking part in the Clock Carriers' Way scheme.

SOME USEFUL WORDS AND PHRASES
FOR RAMBLERS

For non-German speaking ramblers we have compiled a brief list of some of the more common words and phrases you're likely to meet or need in the Black Forest. For those with some knowledge of German, you will find that there are certain words and phrases included which are particularly characteristic to this region.

ON THE ROUTE

Barrier	die Schranke
Beware of the dog!	Vorsicht, bissiger Hund!
Clock	die Uhr
Clock carrier	der Uhrenträger
Colours used to mark routes:	
red, blue, green, yellow	röt, blau, grün, gelb
black, white	schwarz, weiß
Cross (religious)	das Kreuz
Grape	die Traube
High-level route	der Höhenweg
Farmhouse	der Bauernhof
Footpath	der Pfad
Road	die Straße/Gaße
Fir tree	die Fichte
Forest path	der Waldweg
Link Path	der Zugangsweg
Major Route	der Hauptweg
Meadow, field	die Wiese
Pine tree	die Tanne
Waymark (diamond-shaped symbol)	die Raute
Stage of the route	die Etappe
Traverse Route	der Querweg
No Entry	Eintritt Verboten
Waterfalls	die Wasserfälle
Vineyards	die Reben
Map	die Landkarte
River	der Fluß
Lake	der See
Bridge	die Brücke
Fool or jester	der Narr

Fountain or spring	der Brunnen, die Quelle
Half-timbered house	das Fachwerkhaus
Local museum	das Heimatmuseum
Monastery	das Kloster/Stift
Parish church	die Pfarrkirche
Pilgrimage church	die Wallfahrtskirche
Spa town	der Kurort
Swimming Pool	das Hallenbad
Open air swimming pool	das Freibad
Open air museum	das Freilichtmuseum
Tower	der Turm, der Aussichtsturm
Tourist Information	der Fremdenverkersamt
Post office	der Postamt
Postage stamp	die Briefmarke
Postcard	die Postkarte
Good morning!	Grüß Gott!, Guten Tag!, Guten Morgen!
Please...	Bitte
Thank you	Danke schön
Excuse me...	Entschuldigen Sie mir bitte...
Do you speak English?	Sprechen Sie Englisch?
I don't understand	Ich verstehe nicht
Please speak more slowly	Bitte, sprechen Sie noch langsamer
I am lost	Ich habe mich verirrt
Can you help me?	Können Sie mir helfen?
How far is it to...?	Wie weit ist es von hier nach...?
Is this the way to...?	Ist das der Weg nach...?
Straight on	Gerade aus
Left	Links
Right	Rechts

ACCOMMODATION

Rooms	Zimmer
Rooms to let, vacancies	Zimmer frei
Bed	das Bett
Shower	die Dusche
Bath	das Bad
Breakfast	das Frühstück
Dinner	das Abendessen
To eat a snack	Vespern
Lunch	das Mittagessen
Snack menu	die Vesperkarte
Toilets	die Toiletten, der Abort, das Klo (more colloquial, "00")

Ladies	Damen
Gentlemen	Herren
Vacant	Frei
Occupied	Besetzt
Lift	der Fahrstuhl
Telephone	das Telefon
To telephone	Anrufen

I have reserved a room	Ich habe ein Zimmer reserviert
What time is breakfast?	Um wieviel Uhr wird das Früstück
serviert?	
Breakfast is from...to...	Das Frühstück ist von...bis...
What time is it?	Wie spät ist es?
Is this seat/place free?	Bitte, ist der Platz/Sitz frei?
No, this is taken	Nein, der Platz ist reserviert
Yes, it's free	Ja, bitte sehr

FOOD AND DRINK

Meal	das Essen
Menu	die Karte
Soup	die Suppe
Beef	das Ochsenfleisch, das Rindfleisch
Horse-radish	der Meerenrettich
Roast Pork	der Schweinsbraten
Venison	das Reh, der Hirsch
Boiled egg	Gekochtes Ei
Fish	der Fisch
Fruit	das Obst
Trout	die Forelle
Salmon	der Lachs
Veal	das Kalb
Bread	das Brot
Bread roll	das Brötchen
Apple juice with mineral water	die Apfelschorle
Milk	die Milch
Cheese	der Käse
Ice cream	das Eis
Beer	das Bier
Tea	der Tee
Coffee	der Kaffee
Water	das Wasser
Mineral water	das Mineralwasser
Apple (grape, orange) juice	Apfel (Trauben, Orangen) saft
Cherry schnapps	das Kirschwasser
Wine	der Wein

Cream	die Sahne
With cream	mit Sahne
Butter	die Butter
Sugar	der Zucher
Salt	das Salz
Pepper	das Pfeffer
Asparagus	der Spargel
Cauliflower	der Blumenkohl
Tomato	die Tomate
Carrot	die Möhre
Spinach	der Spinat
French beans	die Grüne Bohnen
Gherkins	die Gurken
Onion tart	der Zwiebelkuchen
Potatoes	die Kartoffeln
Green salad	der Grünersalat
Mixed salad	Gemischter Salat
Mushrooms	die Pilze
Mushrooms (chanterelles)	die Pfifferlinge
Apricots	die Aprikosen
Bilberries	die Heidelbeeren
Cherries	die Kirschen
Cranberries	die Preiselbeeren
Pear	die (Williams) Birne
Plums	die Zwetschken, Pflaumen
Raspberries	die Himbeeren
Yellow plums	die Mirabelle
Cake	der Kuchen
Gâteau	die Torte
Pasta	die Nudeln, Spätzle
Chocolate	die Schokolade
Cake and pastry shop	die Konditorei
Did you enjoy the meal?	Hat Ihnen das Essen geschmeckt?
Yes, very much	Ja, sehr
The bill	die Rechnung, Bitte Zahlen

TRANSPORT

Train	der Zug, die Bahn
Express train	der Schnellzug
Stopping train	der Eilzug, der Personenzug
Bus	der Autobus
Bus-stop	die Autobus Haltestelle
Journey	die Fahrt/Reise
Ticket	die Fahrkarte

Single	Einfach
Return	Hin-und-Zurück
Luggage	das Gepäck
Has the luggage arrived yet, please?	Bitte, ist das Gepäck schon angekommen?
Platform	der Bahnsteig, der Gleis (bay)
To change trains	Umsteigen
No smoking	Nicht rauchen
Timetable	der Fahrplan
Departures	Abfahrt
Arrivals	Ankunft
What is the fare to...?	Wieviel kostet es nach...?
From which platform does it leave?	Von welchen Bahnsteig fährt er?
Airport	der Flughafen
One-way street	Einbahn
Taxi	das Taxi
Petrol	das Benzin
Diesel (oil)	das Diesel

GENERAL

Bank	die Sparkasse
Passport	der Reisepass
Currency changing	Geldwächsel
Travellers cheques	die Reisechecks
Doctor	der Arzt
Dentist	der Zahnarzt
Pain	der Schmerz
Hospital	das Krankenhaus
Nurse	die Krankenschwester
Ambulance	der Krankenwagen
Accident	der Ufall
Insurance	die Versicherung
Police	die Polizei
Help!	Hilfe!
Lost	Verloren
Stolen	Gestohlen
I have a toothache	Ich habe Zahnweh
Hayfever	der Heuschnupfen
A cold	der Schnupfen
Headache	die Kopfschmerzen, das Kopfweh
Stomach ache	die Magenschmerzen

111

Heart attack	das Herzanfall
Diabetes	die Zuckerkrankheit, der Diabetes
Allergy	die Allergie
Sunburn	der Sonnenbrand
Sickness, nausea	die Übelkeit
Blister	die Blase
A sprained (ankle, knee)	(der Knöchel, das Knie) verstauchen
Elastoplast, sticking plaster	das Pflaster
Chemist's shop	die Apotheke

Further Reading

Although most English guidebooks on West Germany do have a section about the Black Forest, there is very little which describes the area in detail and even less which caters exclusively for walkers. However, *The Visitors Guide to the Black Forest* by George Wood published by Moorland Press (Hunter New Jersey) provides a useful introductory outline to the region. Furthermore, once you are actually in West Germany you will find that most museums have either a museum guide in English or an English summary, and much tourist information is now available in English.

For readers of German, the *Bild Atlas* series on the central and southern Black Forest (HB Verlag) are excellent value, as are the *Merian* series on the northern and southern Black Forest. *Bild Atlas* (as the name implies) provide excellent road maps to accompany the text, whilst *Merian* has a greater emphasis on more scholarly articles. Both series are superbly illustrated and are widely available in bookshops throughout Germany.

Bild Atlas:	*Mittlerer Schwarzwald (no.55)*
Bild Atlas:	*Südlicher Schwarzwald (no.52)*
Merian:	*Nördlicher Schwarzwald*
Merian:	*Südlicher Schwarzwald*

Rudolf Walz's *Auf dem Weg der Uhrenträger* in the Walz Wanderferien Verlag (Reutlingen) series is a splendid guide to the Clock Carriers' Way for those with fluent German, though it is not always easy to find walking instructions among much interesting cultural detail.